Crappie!

by

Jim Robbins

Mississippi River Publishing Co.
Leland, Mississippi

Text copyright © 1991 by
Jim Robbins

Manufactured in the United States of America
Printed by Taylor Publishing Co. of
Dallas, Texas
Designed and produced by Betsy Harper
CIP data pending
Illustrations by Emily Craig.

10 9 8 7 6 5 4 3 2 1

Mississippi River Publishing Co.
P.O. Drawer 391
Leland, Mississippi 38756

This book is dedicated to the best parents a boy could have, who encouraged me in all of my fishing and hunting endeavors; and to my lovely daughter, Tracey.

CONTENTS

Acknowledgements

This book could not have been written without the contributions made by the following fishermen and manufacturers:

Rich Abdollar - Clinton, Missouri

Jim Abers - Boydton, Virginia

Lewis Barry - Phoenix, Arizona

Charlie Beavers - Harrison, Arkansas

Buddy Boyd - Almo, Kentucky

Charlie Brewer

Sally Carroll - Kuttawa, Kentucky

Steve Carpenter - Louisville, Tennessee

Emily Craig - Phenix City, Alabama

Daiwa

George and Gena Darnell - Kuttawa, Kentucky

Gary and Shane Darnell - Murray, Kentucky

Fisher Marine

Dr. Tom Forsythe - Hardin, Kentucky

Glen Fowler - Melrose, Iowa

Jim Fowler - Tunica, Mississippi

Hubert Griffey - Clarksville, Tennessee

Shorty Grooms - Nashville, Tennessee

Ronnie Guyton - Columbus, Mississippi

Al Hamilton - Hornbeak, Tennessee

Bob Holmes - Trenton, Tennessee

Humminbird

Malcolm Lane - Gilbertsville, Kentucky

Lowe

Lowrance

Sonny Mason - Plum Branch, South Carolina

Al Matura - Chandler, Texas

Dr. Bill Miller, III - Monroe, Louisiana

Bob Monoghan - Camanche, Iowa

Harold Morgan - Nashville, Tennessee

Jimmy Orsborn - Edgewood, Texas

Polar Kraft

Procraft

Joe Rattray - Cedar Bluff, Alabama

Starcraft

Super Jigs

Carneal Walden - Nashville, Tennessee

John Welbern - Hendersonville, Tennessee

Scott Wicker - Eddyville, Kentucky

Foreword

People often ask "You wrote a book about crappie? Nothing else? What can you say about Crappie fishing that would require an entire book?"

Well, the question became irritating, so I quit trying to answer it. I would have been talking to someone who didn't know anything about crappie fishing and I don't like to waste my time with people who lead pointless lives.

But there is an answer and here it is: crappie fishing is a multi-dimensional sport if you pursue it for more than a few months at a time. Some fishermen become one-dimensional when they restrict their efforts to a specific set of circumstances—for instance: the angler who fishes only in the spring when spawners are in shallow water; or a pontoon boat troller on Mississippi River oxbows who gets out only in July and August when fish are suspended in open water; or even an ice fisherman in Wisconsin or Minnesota.

If you're going to maintain this tunnel vision approach to crappie fishing, then this book is not for you. This book is written for the crappie enthusiast who wants to broaden his knowledge of this grand sport; perhaps ply his trade on a new body of water or trek to one of those much publicized crappie havens in another state. Reading *Crappie!* will allow you to do that—or at the very least, help unravel some of the mysteries of your home waters.

To help me in this endeavor, I have solicited advice from true experts about their methods on their respective reservoirs from Arizona to Virginia. I think that any "how-to" book requires input from sources other than the author. After talking to these fellows, I found out right away that I didn't know nearly as much as I thought I did about these "white perch"!

One dimensional!! Ha! Since I've completed the manuscript for *Crappie !* I've already learned of several new techniques that will have to go in Volume II. New methods, ideas, and technology will keep us on our toes in quest of America's favorite fish. Earlier this morning as a group of us sat around Kingston's Bait Shop on Tunica Cutoff, Rich Howe told me a story of a legendary jig he ties which is lethal on big winter crappie in shallow water!

So this book is not the final word, nor all inclusive, but it will help you catch more crappie. If it doesn't, then maybe you should think about taking up golf!!

Jim Robbins
P.O. Box 1887
Tunica, MS 38676

Crappie!

Jim Robbins' Crappie Journal

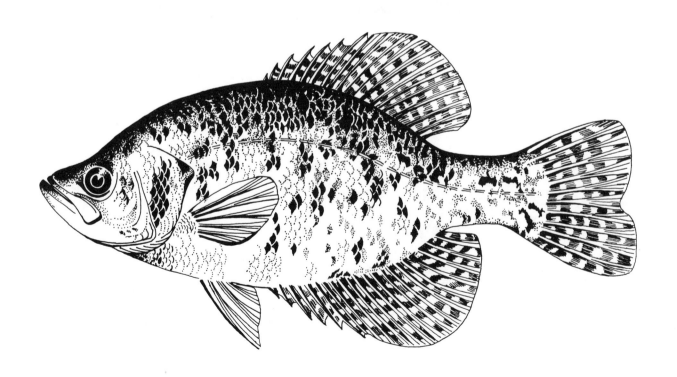

Jim Robbins' Crappie Journal

Life History

Chapter I

The school of crappie suspended lethargically in 12 feet of water in an open expanse of the willow-lined river chute, a former bed of the mighty Mississippi, but now cut off from "Ole Miss" by earthen plugs on both ends that had slowly filled in over the decades. Only during winter and spring floods did the big river add her invigorating influx.

Twice during the coldness of February, and it had been severe by lower Mississippi Valley standards, the school had migrated downstream to the runout leading to the river but they had returned to their winter holding area in the mouth of one of the three creeks feeding the oxbow.

This was the fourth winter for the school which numbered perhaps 100 fish of one to two pounds. Their efforts to spawn the past two springs had been unsuccessful due to high waters which had receded before the eggs hatched and left them dry. The gap in the standing crop would soon be noticed by fishermen.

The short February days were becoming not noticeably longer, but longer. The sun became a direct influence on the movements of the school. When a characteristic warm spell occurred in mid-month accompanied by three days of sunshine, the school shallowed up just below the surface. The new warmth seemed to stimulate other creatures—a five-foot alligator gar swept through the tightly bunched school and injured two of the panfish before grasping a victim in toothed jaws. His demeanor and physique hadn't changed since prehistoric times.

No less a predator than the fearsome gar, but one that had been absent for many years in the Mississippi river bottoms, suddenly appeared and scattered the school again, taking one of the smaller males for a shoreline banquet—a river otter. Yet another member was lost to an aerial strike from a bald eagle—a former resident of the Mississippi Valley which, like the otter, had in recent years returned in sufficient numbers to add an unforgettable splendor to the wildness of the river bottoms. The eagle and his mate had migrated from Canada, following the concentrations of waterfowl down the flyway, preying primarily on weak or crippled ducks. But he couldn't resist an easy fish dinner when he saw the school sunning near the surface. The fish the raptor selected was bigger than anticipated and he had to exert a great deal of energy to lift the two-pounder back to his dead snag.

These predations, though disrupting, were natural and the school would persist in spite of them if other disasters could be averted such as farm chemical pollution or a third straight year of lost spawn. It would take years to rebuild the oxbow back to its former productivity.

A cold front sent the crappie deeper but urges were stirring that had been long dormant. Winter was wearing down. The school became more restive and scattered. They sensed that changes were imminent. A warm rain the first of March provided the stimulus they had been waiting for; a second, heavier rain followed by a third sent the rising chute into new ground as it spread through the flat bottomlands and over beaver dams into nearby corn and soybean fields.

After three days of high water, the school, which had remained loosely intact, left the deep water safety of the tributary to scatter and prowl for food in the inundated territory. For a week, they fed on crustaceans, minnows, aquatic insects and then began to search for spawning sites. Water temperatures were warming fast.

A fortuitous fall in the flood crest the next day prevented, at least for the present, a recurrence of the past two years. Able to sense the slightest change in water levels, the crappie began moving back to drainage ditches and sloughs. Natural obstructions to the receding waters such as duck blinds, beaver dams and log dams became prime feeding stations for the voracious panfish who waited in ambush in the eddies. One obstruction threatened the entire school when a fast-falling river almost marooned them behind a beaver dam. Only a small rivulet near the center was deep enough for them to ford the barrier. A number of large carp were also stranded and they were helping keep the gap open by flapping their heavy bodies across one by one. The thrashing of scales and tails attracted an interested spectator who quickly decided to join in the fun—a raccoon. He grasped and wrestled with three or four giant carp to no avail and much to his disappointment, when his dexterous paws wrapped around one of the smaller crappie. With experience born of working under the water for frogs and crawfish, he flipped the fish onto the beaver dam where it was finally dispatched.

As "Ole Miss" withdrew, so did the crappie—back into their tributary. Downstream, the migrating fish encountered another obstacle—one more formidable this time as the illegal size meshes of a fish poacher's net stretched across the mouth of the narrow creek captured the big crappie by the dozens. A number of them jumped instinctively over the top to safety. Only about half of the school that had started the winter was left.

By the last of March, the oxbow stabilized for the time being and the school dispersed into the shallows to spawn around cypress knees, fallen logs, brush, duck blinds and treetops. Snapping turtles, anchored in the mud, picked off an easy meal from time to time before the females returned to deeper water. Spawning was successful. Stable water conditions produced a bumper crop of fry—enough to withstand the rigors of predation and natural disasters and to provide a productive base for succeeding generations.

This scene is replayed every year in all of the old chutes, sloughs and oxbows connected to major rivers such as the Missouri, Mississippi, Arkansas, Ohio, Black Warrior and others. It is also replayed in all other types of crappie waters in different degrees. A crappie in Ontario's Lake of the Woods or Chautauqua Lake in New York may not have to fend off an alligator gar but he does have to occasionally dodge a muskie or northern pike! And while a crappie in southwest lakes may not face any of these predators, he still stands to lose his life in the jaws of a striped bass or largemouth bass! In fact, the introduction of striped bass into Nevada's Lake Mead and Lake Mohave has spelled doom for these once fertile crappie waters.

The poor crappie is comparable to the lowly rabbit......everybody wants to eat him for dinner. And they do. It's a wonder of nature that any survive, especially considering the inroads man makes on their populations. More noble gamefish (bass, trout, pike, muskie) all have their devotees who release those that are caught. Do crappie fishermen practice catch and release? The obvious answer is no because I had never seen anybody release a crappie until recently. But yes, there are now a few who do release some of their crappie. And believe it or not, the practice can be beneficial to the fishery. Perhaps the most important benefit comes during the spring spawning season. Depending on body weight, a female crappie, either black or white, may deposit 7,000 to 200,000 eggs in a sand or gravel nest fanned out by the male black crappie or on roots and limbs of bushes and trees in the case of white crappie.

After egg laying, the females depart, leaving the parental chores to the male who must fan the eggs to insure their hatching. Remove the male and the eggs will either be covered with a destructive fungus or eaten by small fish. The male is the key to a successful spawn. Therefore, when fishing during the traditional spawning season and you know or feel sure crappie have spawned, return the males to their nest guarding duties and seek out the females in deeper water.

How will you know if the females have spawned? One of three ways: (1) if you caught females on the last trip and now are catching only males—simple deduction; (2) by word of mouth from fellow fishermen, a reliable marina operator or the local baitshop; and (3) by taking the water temperature—crappie spawn, depending on the body of water, in a temperature range of 56° to 68°. Black crappie tend to spawn on the cooler end of this scale (56°-64°F) and white crappie in the 64° to 68° range. This is a majority range......there are exceptions and your favorite lake may be one of them. I'm sure that crappie spawn in water temperatures in Minnesota and Canadian lakes that would be

Oxbow Diary

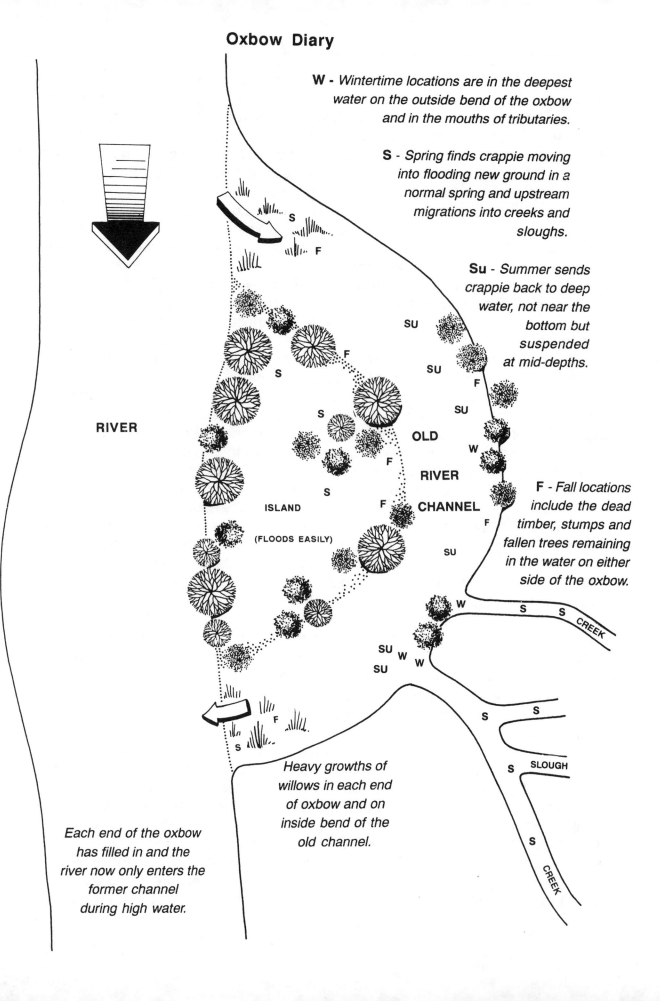

W - Wintertime locations are in the deepest water on the outside bend of the oxbow and in the mouths of tributaries.

S - Spring finds crappie moving into flooding new ground in a normal spring and upstream migrations into creeks and sloughs.

Su - Summer sends crappie back to deep water, not near the bottom but suspended at mid-depths.

F - Fall locations include the dead timber, stumps and fallen trees remaining in the water on either side of the oxbow.

RIVER

OLD

RIVER

CHANNEL

ISLAND

(FLOODS EASILY)

CREEK

SLOUGH

CREEK

Each end of the oxbow has filled in and the river now only enters the former channel during high water.

Heavy growths of willows in each end of oxbow and on inside bend of the old channel.

too cold for midwestern and southern crappie. Applying the temperature rationale requires a knowledge of spawning behavior which enables the erudite angler to focus on deeper water females when the water temperature in the shallows is too warm.

Water temperature is a reliable indicator of spawning behavior in the spring.

This is the first of many times throughout this book that I'll mention an exception to a general rule. There are always going to be exceptions because too many factors play a role in the biological and physical make-up of any body of water. Plus, there just doesn't seem to be any axioms relating to crappie fishing that are 100% true......with the possible exception that they will be in water! All others are fallible and subject to change!

Let me make one more point about catch and release to illustrate another trait of crappie......they are slow growing and short lived! In the middle latitudes of the country, Missouri for instance, it takes three growing seasons for a crappie to reach nine inches! And this is under optimum conditions. In regions north of Missouri, the growth rate is slower on the average and greater in states south of the "Show Me" state. For example, in Texas, crappie are found to grow seven to eight inches in one growing season! An eight-inch crappie weighs around four ounces and an 11-inch crappie weighs close to a pound. Sexual maturity is reached during the second or third summer and normal life expectancy is three to four years although some specimens have been known to live as long as eight years. Therefore, to remove a crappie in the "slab" category (over one pound) is to remove a fish producing those hundreds of thousands of eggs necessary to perpetuate the species.

But is such conservation necessary? A basic law of Mother Nature is that she produces offspring far in excess of what is actually needed to maintain the species. This is especially true in the world of fish where a minute number of fry hatched ever reach maturity.

Fishery biologists tell us that a boom year in catching good sized fish may have been the result of an actual bad spawning year! Dr. Tom Coon of the University of Missouri says that too many crappie can deplete their own food supply and several successful spawns may produce poor fishing. The ideal situation may be where crappie have a good spawn every other year.

Dr. Tom Forsythe, a biologist with the Tennessee Valley Authority at the Land Between the Lakes, makes a similar prognosis. An overabundance of spawn can result in overpopulation, producing stunted crappie. Stunting is caused by insufficient food supplies. Specifically, the carrying capacity of the lake is exceeded. When the hatches are less than successful, there is less competition for food and the fry grow faster and are less susceptible to predation. The end result is a year in which a lot of good fish are taken by anglers.

According to Dr. Forsythe, zooplankton is the basis for young fish survival. Zooplankton are minute organisms that are the food and nourishment for newly hatched fry during the early months of their existence. A lake rich in zooplankton can support a larger and healthier population of crappie than those that don't. Science has by and large failed to recognize the importance of zooplankton in determining the causes of lake and reservoir problems.

For years, fishermen in Texas complained to the Texas Parks and Wildlife Department about the quality of crappie fishing in many of their lakes. The lakes were full of stunted crappie and there were too many "lean" years and not enough "good" years.

Upon investigation, biologists found that both the stunted fish and "lean" years were the result of overfishing. The crappie weren't stunted, they were actually growing very fast; but they were only a year old! Fishing pressure was removing them before they had a chance to mature! Taking research data from Missouri, Texas biologists decided to try size limits (10-inch minimum) and creel limits (25 fish) on a selected group of lakes. The results have been even more dramatic and positive than the biologists expected.

Other states have followed or are considering a similar route. We have finally realized that even the supposed legions of crappie can be depleted by fishing pressure.

In recent years, fishery biologists have turned their attention to factors and conditions affecting crappie.

*Photo courtesy of TVA's Land
Between the Lakes*

Do you know how biologists found out that fishermen were actually taking over 50 percent and possibly as high as 70 percent of the total population? With no disrespect whatsoever to biologists because I'm one of them, let me say in their defense, that their research and studies are being consumed by the more glamourous species—bass, walleye, trout, striped bass, and others. Nothing much was being done on the lowly crappie—he was always there. Oh, sure, some years were better than others, but not to worry, the crappie would return.

Biologists string a net around a section of shallow water on a Mississippi Reservoir and then apply a solution of rotenone.

The rotenone depletes the oxygen in the treatment area and causes all species to come to the surface where they are scooped up and collected in buckets.

The Counting Table

A team of fishery biologists count and record each specimen taken from a one acre sampling of water which had been rotenoned. The study will indicate the percentage of species and their growth rates.

Keith Meals, Fishery Biologist for Mississippi's Dept. of Wildlife, Fisheries and Parks, displays a healthy "slab" taken in the sample from the fertile waters of Arkabutla Lake in North Mississippi.

The answer to the question is money, or more specifically, money being given out by sponsors of Crappiethon contests that began on a number of southern impoundments in 1986. Crappiethons are discussed in more detail in a later chapter but the premise is to place a numbered tag on several hundred crappie and release them in the lake. For the next 60 to 90 days, anybody catching a tagged crappie can turn in the tag for verification to the nearest marina or baitshop. A tag can be worth thousands of dollars......dollars that are guaranteed by any one of a number of businesses in the lake's area of influence as well as national sponsors such as Johnson reels, Rebel Yell Whiskey, Lowe boats, Mercury Motors, etc.When some of the bigger marinas and resorts agreed to sponsor four or five $5000 fish, they were taking a chance that those fish would not be caught during the Crappiethon time frame. I mean, how could even ONE of those fish be caught? The odds were definitely on the sponsors' side. Even the insurance companies thought so and made the premiums for insurance policies on the big dollar fish relatively low. It may be the last time in insurance history that they are the victims of percentages and their own actuarial tables.

Yes, the whole crappie world (especially insurance companies) was astounded that such a great percentage of the tagged crappie were being redeemed for the cash and prizes. For the first time, biologists and fishermen realized that crappie apparently aren't an inexhaustible resource.

Another sidelight to the Crappiethon phenomena which enlightened or perhaps further mystified our understanding of this fish, concerned movements. Tagged fish released in the vicinity of sponsors (marinas) by Crappiethon officials began showing up 10 to 20 miles away! Bob Maxwell, a good friend of mine who kept detailed records in his role as a Crappiethon director, notes on numerous occasions the long distances between where the crappie was released and where it was finally caught. One in particular stands out......a crappie was released in Poplar Creek on Lake Barkley near Buzzard Rock Resort. This fish traveled downstream seven miles, through a two-mile canal and into Kentucky Lake where the voyager turned upstream and ended up in Malcolm Creek near Moor's Resort, a trip of 14 miles! From these occurrences, we could deduce that perhaps crappie weren't the stay-at-homes we had always thought.

So just who is this fish we call a Crappie? Actually not everybody calls him a crappie. The Fish Nomenclature Committee of the Outdoor Writers Association of America spearheaded a movement a few years ago to adopt an approved list of common names for North American sport fish. Homer Circle, the chairman of that committee, admitted that it wasn't easy because there were 55 common names but in the Deep South, "white perch" is fairly common while in Florida the name "specks" is popular and in Louisiana, the Cajun word "sac-a-lait" is used which means "bag of milk," a tribute to its delicate meat and table quality.

Bob Dennie, editor of the *Louisiana Conservationist*, tells an interesting story of the largest crappie ever caught in Louisiana or, for that matter, the world! In November of 1969, Lettie Robertson was fishing from the bank in the Westwego Canal when she hooked and landed a crappie which was photographed and then weighed on certified scales at six pounds! A new world mark that would best either of the two current record holders in the black crappie or white crappie categories.

Lettie, glad that all the uproar over the catch was finally over, took the fish home and ate it for supper (the same fate suffered by the world record walleye and largemouth bass)! And no doubt by other species whose captors didn't realize what they had caught.

However, Lettie's crappie suffered a worse fate. The photograph could not reveal whether the fish was white or a black crappie and since no bonafide authority had viewed the remains, it could not be recognized as a new world record for either species!

The state of Louisiana didn't understand why there was so much fuss about whether it was black or white, they listed it as the state record sac-a-lait!

Consult any scientific description of the two species of crappie and you'll find both fish are physically the same with one obvious difference besides coloration. The white crappie (*Pomoxis annularis*) has six spines on the dorsal fin and the black (*Pomoxis nigromaculatus*) has seven or eight. Their scientific names give a clue to the difference in coloration. *Pomoxis* is a Greek word meaning "opercle sharp"......obviously not a clue to coloration, but the species name, *annularis* is a Latin word meaning "having rings" and refers to the dark bands or "bars" on the body. *Nigromaculatus* is also Latin and means "black spotted", a reference to an all over pattern of irregularly arranged speckles and blotches.

In November of 1984, another species of crappie was caught in Louisiana by Jimmy Lee Holley while fishing the Corney Creek branch of Lake Darbonne. The fish measured 12 $\frac{1}{8}$ inches in length, weighed one pound, two ounces and was GOLDEN! Not just gold tinted or with a yellow-orange aura, this crappie had a genuine gold color on every part of its body (see photo on page 49).

Folks who didn't believe were then treated to a second golden fish which was caught in the same area by J.W. Sams that measured 12 $\frac{1}{4}$ inches and weighed 1 $\frac{1}{4}$ pounds! Was this fish a new species, perhaps a *Pomoxis goldenii?* No, said Dr. Neal Douglas, ichthyologist at Northeast Louisiana University, these two specimens are merely a rare color phase of the white crappie! Other distinctive traits between the two species appear in their habits and preferences. The black crappie prefers aquatic vegetation, clear water and is less tolerant of turbidity and siltation. It seems to be better adapted to the cooler climes of more northern waters while the white crappie holds forth in the Southern tier of states with the exception of Florida. Most states enjoy an overlapping of the two ranges and the biology of reproduction is practically the same. Growth in length of the black crappie is usually less than that of the white crappie, even in the same waters. However, the black crappie is generally heavier per inch and is a much more robust opponent on the end of a line.

Most of this country's reservoirs were built in the 40s and 50s and many of these have been dingy throughout their life due to the constant washing of clay and mud banks. By now, however, the soil is gone, leaving a gravel or rocky substrata which creates clearer water conditions. With the clearer water has come an influx of aquatic vegetation that seems to favor the black crappie over the white.

As the lakes have changed their character, so must the crappie fisherman change his. He can no longer charge into shallow water, drop a minnow on a big cork into the prevailing cover and expect to catch the crappie he once did. He now has to lay off the cover and flip a jig or cast a minnow to wary crappie.

Forget small waters when you consider crappie fishing......ponds and creeks rarely entertain much of a crappie population. They do best in the big impoundments, major rivers or large natural lakes where there is an ample supply of forage.

Black Crappie
Pomoxis nigromaculatus

7 to 8 dorsal spines

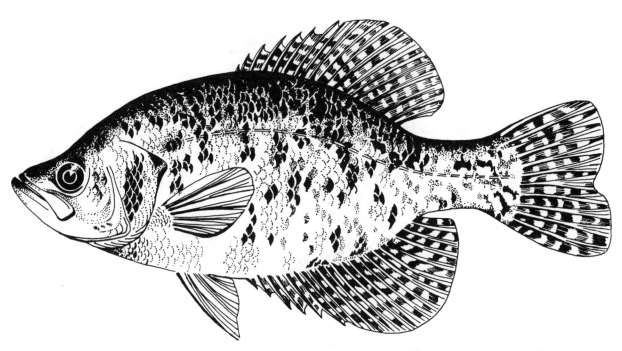

Heavily mottled sides

CHARACTERISTICS.................. Heavier in the body than a White crappie of equal length. Anal fin as long and large as the dorsal fin and with 6 spines.

COLORATION........................... Black speckled sides, a dark olive back with emerald and purple iridescence. Tail, dorsal, and anal fins appear to be black with white spots.

RANGE..................................... Extends further north than the white crappie. Good populations of big black crappie are found in Manitoba's Star Lake and Ontario's Lake of the Woods. Dominates in the northern U.S. because it seems to prevail in clear, weedy waters.

HABITS.................................... More abundant in the clearer tributaries of reservoirs where they are fond of standing timber and stumps as well as aquatic vegetation.

White Crappie
Pomoxis annularis

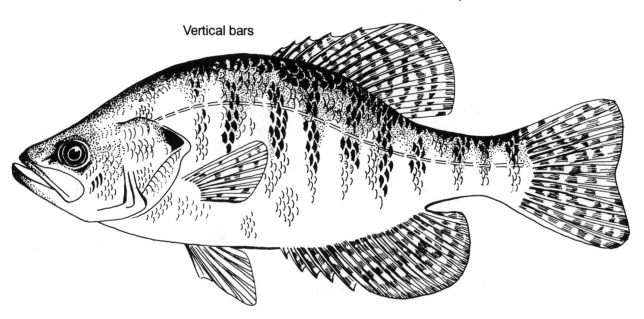

5 to 6 dorsal spines

Vertical bars

CHARACTERISTICS.................. *Begins nesting activity when water temperatures rise over 55 degrees. Spawning sites can be located in water depths ranging from a few inches to 20 feet.*

COLORATION........................... *Dark olive back with silvery sides marked with dark vertical bars. Colors vary in intensity with the clarity of the water. Males turn much darker during spawning and are often thought to be Black crappie.*

RANGE.................................... *Found in most of the U.S. with the possible exception of Maine and Idaho. More prevalent in the Midwest and Southern states.*

HABITS.................................... *Prefers to relate to woody structures (brush, timber, logs, stumps) in the spring and fall but often suspends in open water during the summer and winter. Gizzard shad and threadfin shad are the dominant food items although other small fish, aquatic insects (esp. Mayflies), and small crustaceans are on the menu.*

Equipment

Chapter II

Time was when all you needed to catch a mess of crappie was a cane pole, cork, split shot, and a lively minnow......from the bank! Or at the most, from a wooden jon boat sculled around flooded willows and trees. Those were the good old days! Ah, sweet memories. When crappie were crappie and fishermen were all men!

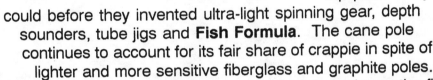

Well, don't despair, those good old days are still here although 1988 was certainly an off-year. You can catch just as many crappie today with that simple equipment as you could before they invented ultra-light spinning gear, depth sounders, tube jigs and **Fish Formula**. The cane pole continues to account for its fair share of crappie in spite of lighter and more sensitive fiberglass and graphite poles.

Lew Childre of Foley, Alabama brought out the first 10- to 14-foot fiberglass poles. Some models were one piece but others were sectional and slipped into a base section only four feet long......a big advantage for transporting in cars which were becoming smaller anyway. Plus, it was easier to sneak away from your neighbor if you didn't have to tie a bundle of canes to the top of the car......a sure giveaway!

Other innovations included a reel built into the butt of the pole with the line running through the center and a pole with line guides and a reel seat suited for practically any kind of reel. All it had to do was hold line. Fly, spinning or spin-cast reels worked equally well.

Line guides and reels allow the angler to grab the line when hung up, pull it taut and jab the tip of the pole into a jig to dislodge it from its captor. The disadvantage is that fixed line guides prohibit the telescoping feature unless sliding guides are used and they're always sliding at the wrong time. A compromise developed by Ronnie Guyton of Columbus, Mississippi, one of the best crappie fishermen in the Magnolia state, involves a telescoping pole with one guide on the first section and only one other guide on the tip. A Four Rivers line holder is taped to the handle. This outfit permits punching jigs out of brush while breaking down into car storage lengths.

Equipment for successful crappie fishing doesn't have to be elaborate or expensive.

A pole that has become very popular in the last few years is the **"Crappie Stick"** which is made in Jonesboro, Arkansas. It is two-piece with fixed guides on a graphite blank (10 or 11 ft.) and is best matched with a spinning reel.

Bob Holmes uses a "crappie stick" on Kentucky Lake which is big, wide-open water featuring deep dropoffs, stump rows, brushpiles and shoreline brush, and Reelfoot Lake, which is shallow all over and filled with millions of stumps, cypress trees, and acres of aquatic weeds. To fish Reelfoot, Holmes rigs his "crappie stick" with a small Carlisle cork, split shot and minnow. In the fall, he locates small stumps (they produce better than larger ones) and stick-ups around which he dips a $1/16$-ounce tube jig. He tries to hold the jig motionless beside the object until a crappie decides to hit. Hardly does he ever need more than four feet of line on the "Earthquake Lake."

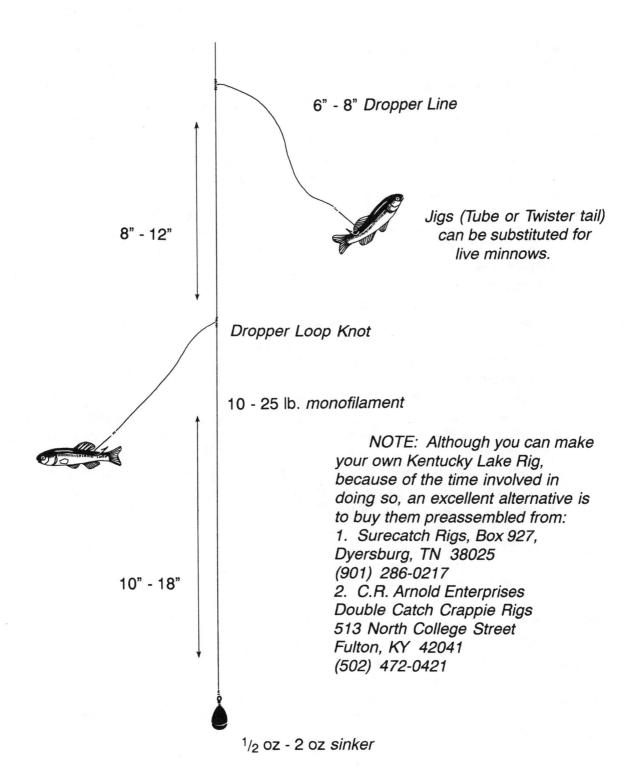

6" - 8" *Dropper Line*

*Jigs (Tube or Twister tail)
can be substituted for
live minnows.*

8" - 12"

Dropper Loop Knot

10 - 25 lb. *monofilament*

*NOTE: Although you can make
your own Kentucky Lake Rig,
because of the time involved in
doing so, an excellent alternative is
to buy them preassembled from:
1. Surecatch Rigs, Box 927,
Dyersburg, TN 38025
(901) 286-0217
2. C.R. Arnold Enterprises
Double Catch Crappie Rigs
513 North College Street
Fulton, KY 42041
(502) 472-0421*

10" - 18"

$1/2$ oz - 2 oz *sinker*

KENTUCKY LAKE TIGHTLINE RIG

The reverse is true on Kentucky Lake where schools of crappie are found on the "drops" in 12- to 25-feet of water. Holmes doesn't change poles but he does change his terminal rig to one developed on this great crappie haven by an old fishing guide. It's a tightline rig consisting of two gold aberdeen hooks tied at different depths on dropper lines above a one- to two-ounce bell sinker. Tightlining is the ultimate method when crappie are holding near the bottom on structure. It became popular on Kentucky Lake as a means of locating and staying on top of dropoffs, years before sonar was to make its appearance.

In recent times, the search for a lighter, more sensitive pole with the strength to lift a slab crappie out of the brush while providing good play with the fish has many crappie addicts reverting to an ancient standby—the fly rod! I first saw guide Steve McCadams use a fly rod for crappie fishing on Kentucky Lake one day when he was showing Terry Madewell and me his deep water techniques. We were probing one of the hundreds of dropoffs in the mouth of the Big Sandy river. Steve had "sweetened" many of them with brush during the winter and they are a favorite summer residence for the white perch!

With a bass action fly rod and a single action reel loaded with monofilament, Steve worked his tightline rig along the edge of a dropoff. The heavy sinker put a slight bow in the rod tip that telegraphed every message from the lake bottom below. It also telegraphed up a number of crappie and a couple of acrobatic channel catfish.

George Darnell and his wife Gena employ a similar style on nearby Lake Barkley where their spare time is spent jigging brushpiles anchored in bays and along dropoffs. George may have been the first to adapt the fly rod to crappie fishing. He got started on Kentucky Lake in the early 60s with a venerable 8 1/2-foot **Heddon Pal**! What a classic! With a sliding cork and a lip-hooked minnow, George and Gena would lower the frantic minnow into the smallest hole in the branches and winch out a big slab.

The proper weight fly rod will have enough backbone to lift a flopping, fighting two-pounder straight up out of the brush and into the boat. The Darnells feel that an 8 1/2-foot rod is as long as you need in heavy cover.

So far, all we've talked about has been the traditional long poles or adaptation of the fly rod but there's a quiet revolution taking place in ultra-light equipment. And for good reason......it's FUN!

Select a graphite spinning rod with ceramic guides and a fast tip. Length is negotiable although the longer rods (6- or 6 1/2-ft.) seem to throw farther with less effort. Graphite's sensitivity gives an angler the confidence that he can feel a crappie swim by his lure! Rods may have reel seats or they may have a "Tennessee Handle" which is a slick handle requiring the reel to be taped on with electrical tape.

REELS

Be sure and select a reel to complement the rod, not overpower it. The outfit has to be balanced......a heavy spinning reel or even a medium weight just won't work on an ultra-light rod. To throw light, you've got to go light. Only a quality ultra-light reel will handle four-pound-test line and $1/32$-ounce jigs!

All of the reel manufacturers produce excellent ultra-light reels. Two companies (**Johnson** and **Zebco**) are producing top-notch spincast reels designed for crappie fishing.

Johnson's Tangle-Free and Country Mile models feature a unique Drive Train drag system and CamDrive gears to eliminate line twist and boost retrieve power. The Crappie Pro reel has an over-sized ceramic line guide for casting light lures.

Zebco's Crappie Classic and UL-3 Classic reels are perfect for casting diminutive jigs and spinners. The UL-3 comes spooled with four-pound line while the Crappie Classic is wound with six-pound test. Both reels have a higher gear ratio (UL-3—4.1:1, Crappie Classic—3.6:1) than the Johnsons (Country Mile—2.92:1, Crappie Pro—2.92:1).

Another innovative reel in major use by crappie fishermen, especially those using fly rods and jig poles where heavy overhanging vegetation demands underhand flipping, is the underslung spincast reel. Zebco and Daiwa feature a reel of this nature while Johnson produces a similar yet different version.

Daiwa's Under Spin Reel mounted on a Daiwa Crappie Pole—a great combination for wade fishing or lowering a lure into heavy cover.

Zebco's UL-4 Classic TriggerSpin features brass gears, straight line drag, 4.1:1 gear ratio and 90 yards of four-pound line. I've used one of these reels extensively on an ultra-light five-foot spinning rod for flipping in close underneath overhanging limbs, piers and boathouses. It's an even better choice on fly rods or long poles when used for flipping or pitching a jig around heavy cover.

Johnson's Crappie Spin Uni-Spin reel differs in that it comes as a built-in rod and reel combination with a thumb-button line release on top of the rod handle. The rod is an ultra-light five-foot fiberglass with ceramic guides and the reel is spooled with 6-pound Stren. In addition to flipping underneath overhangs, this outfit is tops for lobbing a minnow and cork to shallow water brushpiles and weedbeds.

Another method does involve medium weight spinning gear. In the spring when crappie are in clear, shallow water around stumps and brushpiles and it's impossible to get close, put a cork and minnow (or jig) on spinning or spin cast equipment and throw it beyond the target. Reel it haltingly back to the woody cover and let it stay there until a crappie decides to move it. This technique is effective in the spring and again in the fall when the water's too clear to allow a closer approach.

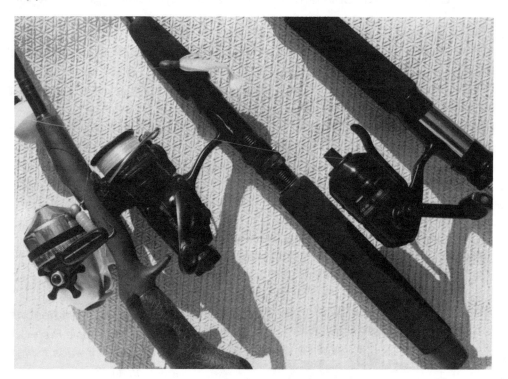

AT LEAST THREE!

There simply is no way that ONE rod and reel or pole is going to fill the needs of a crappie fisherman. After all, no other product in modern times is perfect for all situations, so why should fishing be any different? The absolute minimum is **THREE**! And it is an extremely wise fisherman who has a back-up outfit for each of those three!

Unless you're going to fish one specific way in one specific season at one specific lake, you'll need three outfits. Number one, get an ultra-light and discover the joys of catching slab crappie on feather weight tackle. Try a fly rod for the same reason......it's just a long ultra-light which allows working around standing timber and over brushpiles when casting isn't practical or desirable.

Medium weight spincasting gear has its place when lobbing a cork and minnow or fishing after dark under the lanterns. It's also good for tightlining dropoffs with the Kentucky Lake rig and for trolling with small plugs.

For those times that you need a 12-foot pole to dip back into heavy brush, don't forget a telescoping fiberglass job! It can also be used in traditional trolling and spider-rig trolling, except you can't use just one! Both methods require six or eight poles to be in use at the same time!

Each person's needs will vary according to the type of water being fished but if you're going to a strange lake, take along these three types of tackle and you'll be able to cover any condition.

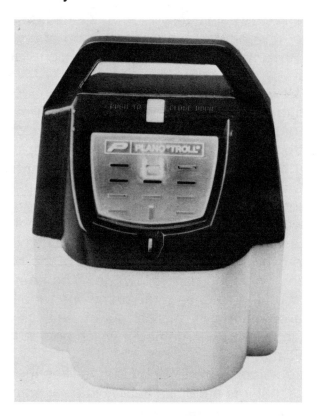

Plano *has added a new feature to their popular trolling minnow bucket......a lockable door. With minnows selling for ten cents apiece, crappie anglers can ill afford to feed a family of raccoons or cats when left out overnight!*

Another innovation includes a reshaped handle to withstand fast starts and to plane easier while trolling. The solid one piece handle gives added strength to a minnow bucket designed with the crappie troller in mind.

LINE

Two observations about line......use a good premium monofilament and consider the use of golden fluorescent or "yellow" line! Yellow is much more visible to the angler which permits the detection of the lightest of strikes and, most importantly, crappie don't seem to notice. At least, not in slightly stained water.

Bass, on the other hand, are a different story and I don't fish a yellow line except at night. In my mind, I believe that a bass can see yellow line and refuse to hit and in that same mind, I'm convinced that it makes no difference in catching crappie!

Back in the 70s when I was a field tester for the Garcia Corp., they sent me a questionnaire asking for my opinion on the introduction of a yellow line. I replied emphatically that there was no place for such a high-visibility line on the American fishing scene!

Boy, was I wrong! However, it took some heavy duty instruction from expert crappie fishermen to convince me otherwise. Guide Tim Harton of Cedar Bluff, Alabama was one of the first to demonstrate his line-watching capability on Lake Weiss. Tim not only guided, but regularly won crappie tournaments with his golden line and homemade weedless jigs. He caught most of his fish suspended over dropoffs and highspots as the jig with a three-inch twister-tail grub fell through the school. The only noticeable sign of the strike was a slight "tick" sideways! Only a yellow line can provide that information!

Allen McBride of Marianna, Arkansas is another who helped make me a believer. Allen fishes the oxbows and backwater lakes of the Mississippi River with a fly rod, tube jigs and 17-pound test yellow line! The heavy line doesn't seem to affect his production (he catches three to my one) and he doesn't lose any jigs. His outfit also allows him to lift a "slab" out of the thick cover he normally fishes and to handle a bully largemouth which gets in the way of the crappie quite a bit of the time!

Not all fishermen are so convinced. Bob Holmes likes the yellow line in dingy water but maintains that it is a definite liability in clear water. He prefers a low visibility monofilament in 4-pound test if the lake is clear, after a cold front, and in the winter. Of course Bob is right, because he believes that the line will turn off reluctant crappie and he wouldn't fish with the same confidence if he had to fish with a high visibility line. Confidence in your presentation catches fish. The bassin' fraternity has been espousing that for years. It also applies to all other forms of fishing.

Whatever your choice, develop a habit of line watching and start catching more crappie!

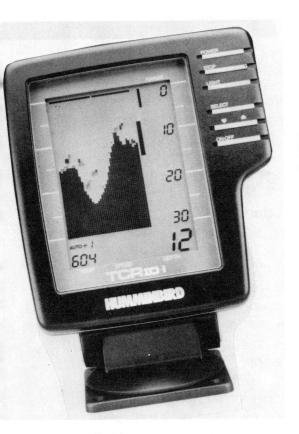
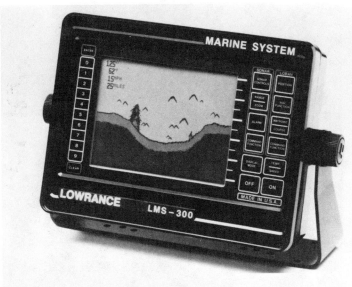

Depth Finders

Chapter III

Today's crappie fisherman has to have some sort of depth indicator if he is to successfully fish beyond the spring spawning season. Exceptions occur when an angler grows up with a lake that was perhaps impounded as he watched or the lake may have a shallow, uniform depth as many natural lakes do. And maybe he's fishing in Louisiana where a boat paddle serves as a depth indicator!

However, take this fisherman out of his home territory and he'll quickly see the need to have an underwater set of eyes! In fact, one set may not be enough. A combination of two is ideal......one on the console and one on the trolling motor. Some fishermen have three......a flasher on the console for high speed running to the fishing area, a graph on the console for pinpointing the structure and a Liquid Crystal Recorder on the trolling motor to stay on top of the breakline.

When Carl Lowrance began marketing his "green box," he literally opened up a new world of crappie angling. He added the rest of the year to the traditional two or three months of spring spawning activity.

Hubert Griffey of Clarksville, Tennessee, sees no reason to use anything other than his "green box."

Fishermen that used to take up golf when crappie returned to deep water could now follow those movements with the new sonar equipment......a technology originally developed by the U.S. Navy for submarine warfare in WWII. Instead of pinging off enemy subs, the sound waves could be bounced off a lake bottom to tell the viewer how deep the water was and when it got deeper or shallower. This was the "missing link" to year-long crappie fishing. Anglers who often used a boat anchor to probe for a change in bottom contour could now turn a knob on the "green box" and look directly into a previously unknown world! Depth changes seemed to be where crappie usually congregated. When the flashing light in the "green box" signaled a change, a marker was thrown overboard......a stick, bottle, oil can, anything!

Some of the best crappie fishermen that I know still swear by the "green box!"

Due to the demand for the boxes and the necessity to mark the dropoff once it was found, marker buoys were designed for this purpose. They are indispensable and worth the additional expense over homemade markers. Choose the hard plastic type with a heavy cord and an adequate weight. The amount of current will dictate the proper amount of weight.

Always have at least three markers in your boat and sometimes you'll need four or five......especially if you're like me and forget to pick them up! An irregularity in the breakline is usually where the crappie will be and it may require a number of markers for a good outline.

I've circled around and around a piece of structure and been completely mystified as to how it lay until I put out markers. Usually the mystery is then cleared up but I'm forced to wait awhile before fish will bite because I've disturbed the water so much. This is something I see other anglers overdoing quite a bit......they'll zigzag back and forth, up and down before being satisfied with their marking effort. Sometimes this may not make a difference but I believe it does most of the time......especially on slab variety crappie. They are not going to let you crisscross over their heads without moving. So try to mark the ends of the dropoff in order to have a good fishing line between the two and keep buoy dropping and boat circles to a minimum.

Markers and maps, which we'll discuss later, are essential accessories to the depth sounder. With a thorough knowledge of how to use them together, success with crappie will be forthcoming.

Flasher type depth machines are as accurate and functional as ever and every boat should have one. However, new technology in the form of LIQUID CRYSTAL RECORDERS has made it easier to determine what is happening on the screen. If flashers have one fault, it is an angler's inability to interpret the oscillating light when fish are close to brush or suspended in submerged trees and under schools of shad. A lot of time is therefore wasted marking off and fishing sections of dropoffs that may not be holding fish. LCRs save valuable fishing time by depicting the presence of fish doubtlessly and accurately. A pass down a long creek channel dropoff or breakline eliminates the barren stretches. Paper graphs satisfy these requirements but they have the disadvantage of running out of paper at the wrong time. LCRs offer the best of both worlds in a single unit by providing other features such as a fish alarm, water temperature reading, stop screen, zone depth gauge, and more. The Humminbird 4-ID goes as far as to identify the fish in "RED!" Subsequent technology will no doubt decipher the species, its age, sex and the time of its last meal! Videos are not only on the horizon, they are infiltrating the ranks.

When purchasing a depth unit, select a namebrand and follow the instructions provided to install the transducer. On aluminum boats, the transducer is normally mounted on the transom because it doesn't shoot through aluminum very well. My preference on fiberglass hulls is to mount the transducer on the inside of the boat. Place it on the layer in contact with the water. If construction will permit, locate the transducer in the forward part of the boat, perhaps the front livewell. In this position, it's easier to stay on a breakline and you'll be better prepared to fish a sudden change in contour. You simply get an answer about ten feet sooner, which is also important when running across a lake and you leave the safety of a channel unexpectedly or encounter an unknown "high spot!" A good fishing area can be found this way sometimes but I don't recommend it because it's too hard on lower units and small checking accounts!

A forward location of the transducer has the added advantage of being properly placed for another unit to be added on the trolling motor and being able to run both off the same transducer. Because after one depth machine is mastered, it's time to add another to the front deck. However, it's better to purchase another transducer and mount it directly to the trolling motor thereby keeping it separate and eliminating the need for a switch to change from one to the other. Obviously, not everyone will need a depth sounder on the front of the boat because many don't go to the bow of the boat to fish. They either troll or have the trolling motor mounted on the transom.

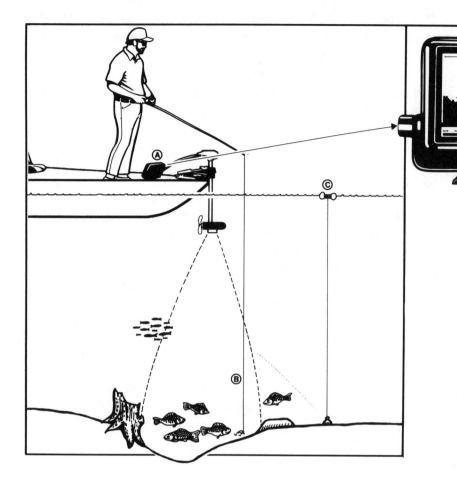

A. A depth finder on the bow and a transducer on the trolling motor allows pinpoint accuracy when fish are holding in a small structure such as a ditch, creekbed, rockpile or a couple of stumps.

Although the depth finder can be mounted on the side of the boat, it's more secure installed on the front deck of the casting platform.

There are different types of transducers so ask for the type specifically designed for use on the trolling motor.

B. Fish straight down in the cone of the transducer and actually feel with your lure whatever is showing up on the screen. You don't need a long pole for this kind of fishing, a light to medium action casting or spinning rod is preferable. Water depth over the structure dictates the choice of lures......if less than 12 feet, a $1/16$ or $1/8$ ounce jig either by itself or in tandem is effective. Deeper water requires a Kentucky Lake rig with minnows, $1/4$ - $1/2$ ounce silver spoons or Little Georges.

C. Marker buoys are indispensable for structure fishing and should be used in conjunction with depth finders. It's just too easy to drift away from a tiny piece of fish-holding cover without the reference point provided by a marker buoy. Being close doesn't count in crappie fishing either— the bait has to be presented in the exact proximity of a potential victim!

If a move is made from the pilot seat to the bow, a depth sounder up there with you will keep you better informed. It enables you to concentrate on staying on top of the breakline without a lot of marker buoys or constant head swiveling to check the sonar device on the steering console, which is always facing the other way anyway! When I have clients in the boat, I can confidently announce "Get Ready" as I come across the breakline holding crappie and have them mentally prepared to receive a strike. The paying customers really like that!

Neither a depth sounder, graph, video, LCR or any combination of the four is a guarantee to successfully catching crappie......not without a great deal of practice. Don't expect miracles. They are merely tools that have to be put into use before you can completely master the information being provided. Study, experimentation and plain ole' fishing will make this your right arm that you won't leave home without!

Fellow outdoor writer Buck Taylor has written the definitive book on depth finders and more recently on Liquid Crystal Recorders. To order a book, contact Buck at P.O. Box 13, Louisville, Alabama 36048 (205) 266-5052.

"There they are! Get Ready!"

For a bow mounted depth sounder, be sure to ask for a transducer that fits on the trolling motor.

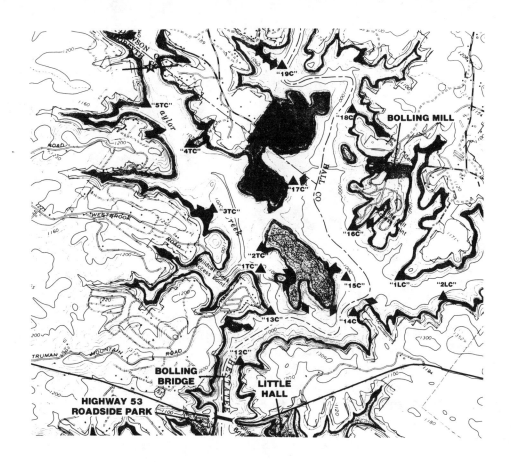

MAPS

Chapter IV

Maps are another important tool to a crappie fisherman, even though he may be intimately familiar with his home lake. A good crappie-producing body of water is usually very large and there's always a potential "honey hole" just waiting to be discovered! Maps can lead to these sweetspots after diligent study and application. Employ the most sophisticated electronic gear in the world and maps will still save measurable amounts of time in deciphering what's down below.

If the basic outline of an underwater contour is known beforehand, a map makes it quicker and easier to mark it off and start fishing. Otherwise, too much time is spent "checking it out" to see where it goes and what it does. One of the most confusing contours on lakes is the "double back", where a creek channel makes a loop and comes almost back to itself. Without a map of this situation, a crappie fisherman will go dizzy trying to see how it lays! And there's no way he'll have enough marker buoys because it'll take about 20! An underwater contour map eliminates the suspense and keeps stress levels down.

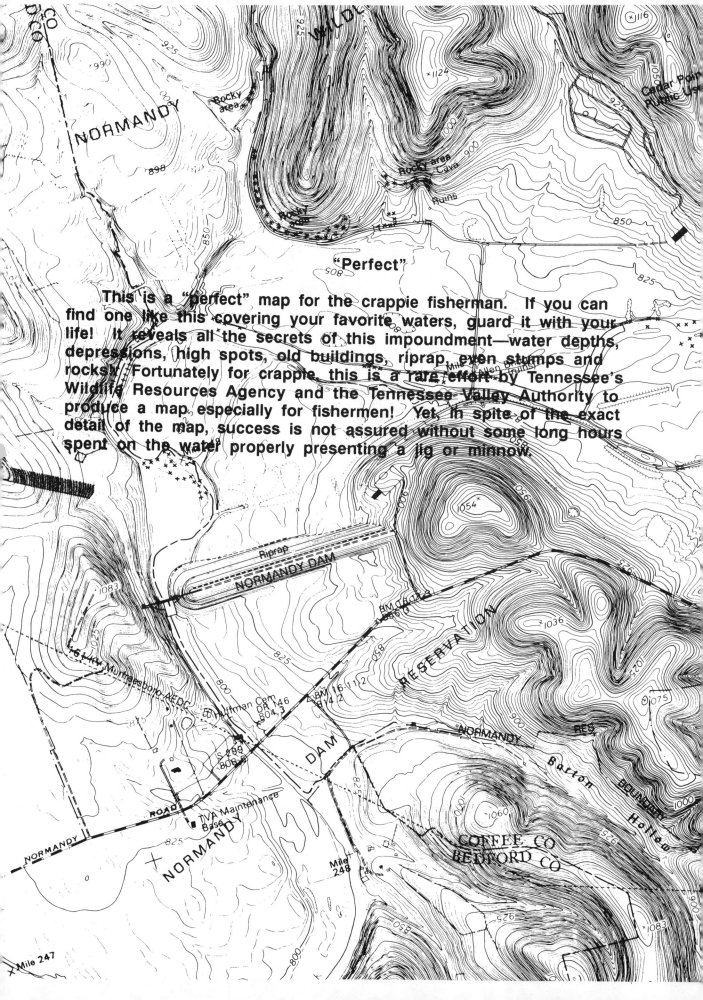

"Perfect"

This is a "perfect" map for the crappie fisherman. If you can find one like this covering your favorite waters, guard it with your life! It reveals all the secrets of this impoundment—water depths, depressions, high spots, old buildings, riprap, even stumps and rocks! Fortunately for crappie, this is a rare effort by Tennessee's Wildlife Resources Agency and the Tennessee Valley Authority to produce a map especially for fishermen! Yet, in spite of the exact detail of the map, success is not assured without some long hours spent on the water properly presenting a jig or minnow.

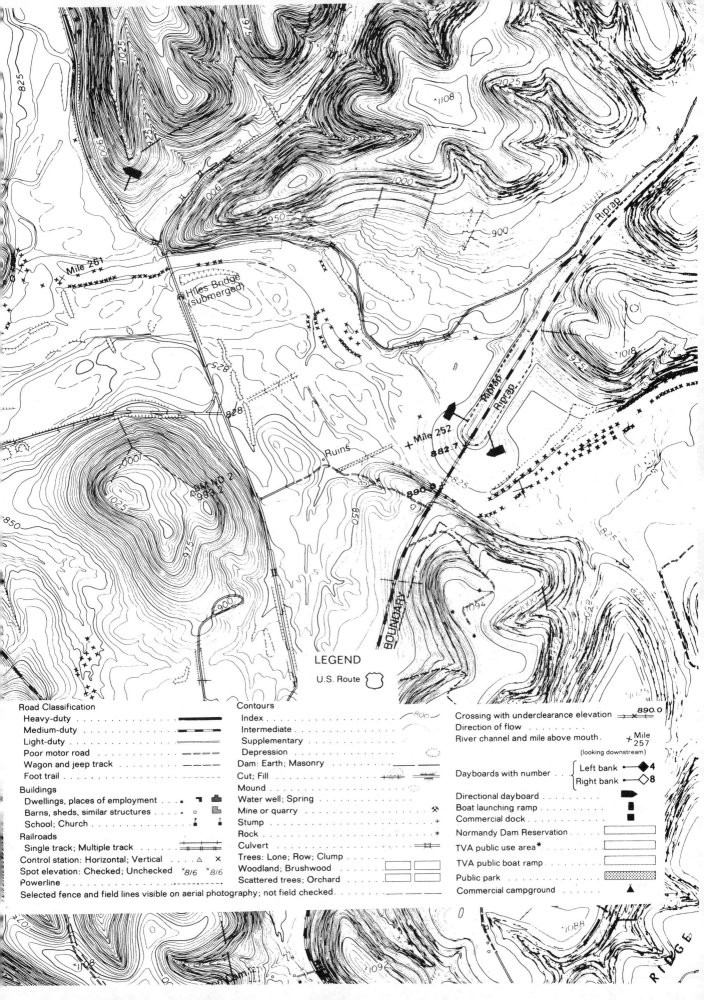

LEGEND

U.S. Route

Road Classification		Contours		Crossing with underclearance elevation	890.0
Heavy-duty		Index		Direction of flow	
Medium-duty		Intermediate		River channel and mile above mouth	Mile 257
Light-duty		Supplementary			(looking downstream)
Poor motor road		Depression			
Wagon and jeep track		Dam: Earth; Masonry		Dayboards with number — Left bank ◆4	
Foot trail		Cut; Fill		Right bank ◇8	
Buildings		Mound			
Dwellings, places of employment		Water well; Spring		Directional dayboard	
Barns, sheds, similar structures		Mine or quarry		Boat launching ramp	
School; Church		Stump		Commercial dock	
Railroads		Rock		Normandy Dam Reservation	
Single track; Multiple track		Culvert		TVA public use area*	
Control station: Horizontal; Vertical		Trees: Lone; Row; Clump		TVA public boat ramp	
Spot elevation: Checked; Unchecked	×816 ×816	Woodland; Brushwood		Public park	
Powerline		Scattered trees; Orchard		Commercial campground	▲
Selected fence and field lines visible on aerial photography; not field checked					

Unfortunately, not all water bodies have been mapped. Dams that proliferated in the late 30s and early 40s were often built before the drainage basin was surveyed by the U.S. GEOLOGICAL SURVEY. Center Hill and Dale Hollow lakes in Tennessee are two that were built in this time period that were unmapped. Both of these, however, are highland types that really don't require a map as much as the lowland reservoirs. The main asset of underwater contour maps of highland reservoirs is the location of "high spots" that come within 20 feet of the surface, thus providing a depth that crappie can relate to.

For a free state index of topo maps, contact the U.S. GEOLOGICAL SURVEY, MAP DISTRIBUTION, BOX 25286, DENVER, COLORADO 80225 (303)236-7477. As good and accurate as the Geological Survey maps are, it can be hit or miss on selecting the desired quadrangle because of their large scale. Invariably, the creek or bay I need the map for is in the corner of four quad sheets!

However, on unmapped lakes, enterprising fishermen usually develop a map based on their experiences and those of others for sale to lake visitors.

Chambers of Commerce, lakeside resorts, baitshops and marinas also often offer a version of a map which are not detailed contour maps but they are, nevertheless, valuable. Birdsong Resort on Kentucky Lake near Paris, Tennessee furnishes their customers a hand drawn map of the winding creek channel leading out to the main lake......a handy reference that contributes to their customers' success and insures return visits. If for no other reason, any kind of map will give an indication of overall size, the best highway approaches, the number and size of tributaries, facilities, access points and nearby towns.

Brochures will do the same thing. The CORPS OF ENGINEERS produces a brochure on each of their 440 projects across the country. They also have excellent maps of many of the rivers, especially the Mississippi River. The Corps is divided into 10 divisions comprised of 37 Districts normally delineated by drainage basins. The 10 Corps division offices are located in Waltham, Mass; New York, Atlanta, Cincinnati, Vicksburg, Chicago, Omaha, Ft. Worth, San Francisco, and Portland, Oregon. Contact the Public Affairs office in those cities (listed under U.S. GOV'T) for maps and brochures of lakes within their division.

Corps' brochures also contain statistical data about the project which give clues to its makeup. The height of the dam indicates whether it's highland (200-300 feet), midland (100-200 feet), lowland (50-100 feet), or canyon (over 300 feet). Surface acres and the number of shoreline miles not only tell the size but indicate how deeply inletted it is with coves. Pool elevations show the extent of winter drawdown and are a reference point for flood stages.

Project Data

Dam
Type...Rolled earthfill
Length, ft. (overall) 10,600
Height, ft. (above streambed) 102
Width, ft. (crown) 30
Width, ft. (base) 800

Spillway
Type... Uncontrolled chute
Crest width, ft..500

Outlet Works
Type...................Single horseshoe conduit, 11 ft. in diameter
Capacity: c.f.s. (cubic feet per second)..........................5,000
Length of conduit, ft..539

Gates
Control: 2 hydraulically-operated slide gates (6 ft. x 12 ft.)
Emergency: (Same as above)

Lake
Elevation, feet above mean sea level:
Top flood control pool...926
Top multipurpose pool..904
Storage, acre-feet:*
Flood control...339,000
Multipurpose and sedimentation..........................213,000
Surface area, acres:
Top flood control pool..21,000
Top multipurpose pool..11,000
Drainage area: (sq. mi.)..549
Shoreline, mi. (multipurpose pool) 180

*One acre-foot equals one acre of water one foot deep or 325,851 gallons.

Impoundment was started November 21, 1969 and the lake filled to the multipurpose level October 10, 1970.

Other agencies BLM, TVA, SCS, and privately owned electric power companies who impound water can be counted on to have a brochure or map. Water supply reservoirs built by city, county and state authorities should also have some sort of map of their endeavors.

The TENNESSEE VALLEY AUTHORITY produces a series of navigation charts in two different sizes and a chart-book form for the Tennessee River which are outstanding to fish by because the underwater contours are extremely accurate. For a TVA map catalogue, contact: TVA, Mapping Services Branch, 200 Haney Building, Chattanooga, Tennessee 37401 (615) 751-MAPS.

For long term use of maps, because they should be in the boat where they will get wet, cover both sides with clear contact paper. Overlap the edges with the contact paper for a waterproof seal.

If you're going to a strange lake, write ahead and get whatever map, brochure or outline on a napkin that will enable you to formulate a game plan and get an image of the lake in mind. It's the same as driving into a strange city; if you look at a map beforehand and visualize how it lays by direction, it's a lot easier to make your way around and not get lost.

A rare color phase of the white crappie...a "Golden Crappie!"

Allen McBride of Mariana, Arkansas prefers "yellow" line on his fly rod outfit for fishing the backwater lakes of the Mississippi River bottoms.

Drink plenty of fluids during a hot summer day and use a good sunscreen lotion.

Fishing piers is an excellent summer pattern but choose those near a breakline for best results.

Docks and piers with sunken brushpiles around them are excellent in the fall.

Night Time

Plastic Bodies

Plastic Bodies

by

Bob Holmes

Chapter V

BEETLES

This is the one that started it all. Beetles were the first plastic imitation to successfully compete with the minnow although the minnow remained the favorite of crappie fishermen after its introduction.

I first fished a $1/8$-ounce Beetle with a #5 split shot under a round Dayton snap-on float 20 years ago on Kentucky Lake. It works as good today as it did then. One day after discovering the Beetle, I accompanied my Dad on a foray in his venerable jon boat on the Big Sandy River. The crappie were in shallow water around buckbrush and were really biting. We'd catch several off of one bush. My Dad was using a minnow on a slip cork and I was experimenting with my new Beetle discovery.

We were pretty competitive about fishing and always trying to stay one ahead of the other. That day belonged to the Beetle! As we approached a likely looking bush, I would take the right side while he took the left. If fish were on the bush, he'd catch one and I'd catch one. But while he was scrambling for another minnow to rebait, I'd be back in the water and have another crappie on the way to the boat. So I was catching two to his one and if he ever dropped his slippery minnow in the bottom of the boat, the ratio widened further.

However, my advantage didn't last; the next time we went fishing, he had a handful of the little **BEETLES!**

Beetles come in multiple leg, double tail, and no-tail versions. All may be fished with a small elbow spinner, or alone. The elbow spinner is ideal for casting in flooded timber, reeds, stumps, and brushpiles in early spring when crappie are in water less than five feet deep. To go deeper, take the spinner off and add a split shot. Use a #7 split shot for fishing in water up to 10 feet deep; a #5 for 10 to 15 feet; and a #3 for 15 to 20 feet.

One of my favorite Beetle methods combats the gooey, green, filamentous algae that prevails in the summer in most lakes. Slip knot a large (#7, #5, #3) split shot to the end of your line. Approximately 18 inches up the line, tie a surgeon's loop. Cut the loop to make a dropper and attach the Beetle. Fish slowly with the rod held high to keep the Beetle moving along above the algae.

TWISTER TAILS

Twister tails, as their name implies, are a great motion bait. The rippling tail gives you a slinky, smooth, swimming movement that is deadly when casting or trolling. Many crappie fishermen prefer them over tube jigs because they can "feel" them better and they also appear to give more visible action in the water.

In winter when fish are deep and after cold fronts when crappie are turned off, a twister tail's slow, regular vibrations can make the difference. Go as light as your equipment can handle. Properly equipped, you should be able to cast a $1/32$-ounce jighead with a one-inch twister tail. This demands a genuine ultra-light outfit with at least four-pound line. Split shot can be added to the line for depth without affecting the tail action.

Winter anglers on lowland and midland lakes seek out creek and river channel ledges which drop from 10 to 35 feet. The dropoff is first outlined with marker buoys and the boat is anchored over and perpendicular to the breakline. Casts are made parallel or at slight angles to the dropoff until a school is located. Cast in a repetitive pattern and count down each cast until encountering cover or fish. Crappie will only hit at a particular depth and concentrating on each cast is the only way to be ready for the slight "tick" when the jig gets in the strike zone. It's slow fishing......but slow only as in reeling and retrieving because huge catches can be made at this time of year with TWISTER TAILS.

At other times, when fish are over brushpiles, stumps, and stakebeds in shallow water, casting a $1/16$-ounce offering is the ticket. Keep the rod tip at a 10 o'clock position and reel slowly and steadily over the structure. Aggressive crappie will come up and inhale the twister tail. If they're not aggressive, experiment with a different retrieve. Stop the retrieve directly over the cover and let the tail work its magic as it falls or give the tail a "shake" with the rod tip.

For working heavy cover for lethargic crappie, select weedless jigheads or **CHARLIE BREWER'S CRAPPIE SLIDER HEADS**. Weedless jigheads come with plastic "Y" guards or multi-strand monofilament fibers......the fewer the strands the better. Charlie's Slider Heads employ a different weedless scheme——he developed an offset hook behind the jighead which allows a soft plastic body to be threaded through the head and onto the offset in the shank of the hook. The point of the hook is then inserted into the body of the grub or twister tail just as you do in rigging a plastic worm Texas-style for bass fishing. You can throw them through a briar patch with a little practice and you won't miss many fish because the hook is embedded if you use a soft plastic. Of course, no weedless jig is 100% weedless or it would also be fishless......so don't take just one weedless jig on a trip, take several!

Charlie Brewer's Crappie Slider Heads and Grubs should be at the local fishing tackle store; if not, they're available through mail-order catalogues such as Cabela's, Bass Pro Shops, and Gander Mountain, or order toll-free 1-800-762-4701.

Another shallow water tactic when crappie are finicky is a twister tail dangled under a slip cork. The constant motion of the tail suspended for a number of seconds over the cover

Charlie Brewer's weedless slider heads

eventually gets the best of the most reluctant crappie. Throw well beyond the target to prevent a fish-spooking splashdown and slowly swim it alongside the stump, treetop or brushpile. This long range presentation is necessary for success when the water is too clear for a closer approach.

The **TWISTER TAIL** is one of those rare angling discoveries, albeit an accidental one, that has revolutionized the sport of fishing.

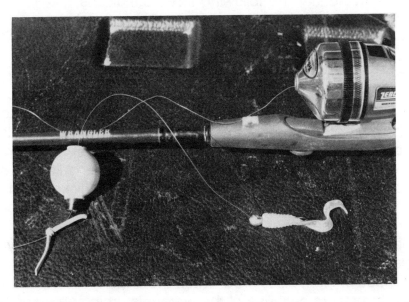

A twister tail under a slip cork is productive in the shallows when the water is too clear for a closer approach.

SHAD BODIES

This group of plastic imitators has a fish-like body with a flattened lobe on the tail which moves from side to side as a result of water pressure.

Shad bodies are effective in dingy water due to the strong vibrations of the club-like tail.

Basically, they represent small minnows or threadfin shad and they are particularly effective under the following three conditions:

(1) *In the late fall and winter* during shad die-offs when sharp temperature changes kill literally millions of shad, the principle crappie forage. Crappie are suckers for minnow/shad imitations one to three weeks after a major die-off. Look for schools of crappie in deep brush and stumps along breaklines and fish super slow!

(2) *During the traditional spring spawn* (March, April, May) after crappie move into shallow water to prepare nest sites. They will not tolerate minnows or other small predators near the site. Fish the spawning territory slowly and thoroughly. Present the shad body with four- to ten-pound line on a heavy action fly rod or fiberglass long pole depending on the thickness of cover and the size of the crappie! Wading is also productive at this time of year by dunking shad bodies around and in bushes, brush, and trees.

In lakes where crappie seem to prefer goldfish minnows, try yellow, orange and gold shades of shad bodies in two-inch sizes.

After periods of high, discolored water, the shad types seem to be more effective than the others because of the water-disturbing ability of the club-like tail which crappie can home in on through vibrations. Fish it around the same heavy cover, but fish a little slower in dingy water.

(3) *In picture book fall weather;* clear skies, stable water stages, warm days (50-70 degrees) and cool (30-40 degrees) nights.

At this time, shallow water warms up rapidly during the day from 11 a.m. to 3 p.m. Threadfin shad migrate to brushpiles, stumps, stakebeds, and treetops and crappie follow.

Practice a slow, quiet presentation with a graphite fly rod. Light line is a must. Fish vertically, directly into the cover. Sometimes one strike will arouse an entire school. If the water's extremely clear, back off and add a small styrofoam float above the jig to pitch a length of line equal to the pole. Or cast a small shad on ultra-light equipment beyond the spooky fish and retrieve it over them.

TUBE TAILS

The tube, with its hollow body and numerous waving tails, is truly a year round lure......it is effective in all four seasons.

The hollow body is the best of the plastic bodies to use with a liquid scent attractant because it acts as a receptacle for a relatively large quantity of potion. Press the body flat with the finger tips. Place the attractant on the open end at the legs. Open and close the fingers to compress the body and suck the liquid into the body. The attractant then oozes off the many tails and releases a scent trail which lasts for a number of casts or dips.

Body sizes vary from $1/64$-ounce (1") to $1/4$-ounce (3") but $1/16$- and $1/8$-ounce sizes are good all around choices. Use the smaller versions ($1/64$, $1/32$) during and immediately after cold fronts. Super Glue applied between the jighead and tube body keeps the tube from slipping and allows more fish to be caught without changing bodies.

Tube tails offer the widest array of color and color combinations in all of the standard, fluorescent, phosphorescent and clear with glitter hues.

Standard colors are: Opaque, generally a milky or cloudy color that doesn't permit the passage of light; Translucent, clear with a color tint that readily permits the passage of light.

Fluorescent colors are those that glow when exposed to natural or artificial light. The intensity of the glow is directly proportional to the intensity of light.

Phosphorescent colors are also activated by natural or artificial light but they continue to glow after the light is removed. These colors are good on dark, gloomy, overcast days, in the deeper depths (15 to 40 feet) and at night.

Clear bodies with colored glitter are the newest and already very popular color options available to the crappie fisherman. Silver, gold, red, blue, and green in single, double and even triple color combinations are fantastic in clear and lightly stained water.

Tube tails provide strikes from reluctant crappie because the multiple tails are always moving enticingly.

OFFENSE AND DEFENSE

After I've selected the type of plastic body to suit the situation, the next decision is to choose a color......no small task when you consider the numbers of colors and color combinations.

Like most crappie fishermen, I have my favorites that I call my "offensive" colors—purple, chartreuse, yellow, pink, and pearl white. These are the ones that I have the most confidence in......my "go to" colors.

All of my other colors are for finicky crappie......those are my "defensive" colors. If my partner is out-catching me with an offbeat color, I should have a similar color that I can resort to. Pick the closest color if you don't have the exact combination. Sometimes close is good enough!

Now, I'm not always smart enough to know what color they'll hit so I rely on a Color-C-Lector to solve the riddles. However, neither is the Color-C-Lector always accurate, but it does give me a starting place and helps eliminate guesswork.

The Color-C-Lector contains three bands for clear, stained and muddy water. Each of the three contains one band recommending six fluorescent colors and one band recommending 26 standard colors. The C-Lector points to one primary standard color and two secondary colors (on either side). One fluorescent color is also indicated at that same position.

Take those four colors and tie them on different poles to see if they'll hit one of them or all four. As I said before, if you don't have the suggested color, try to get close.

Although the Color-C-Lector is a fine piece of equipment, keep in mind that it is merely an aid and not a magical cure-all. With experience and confidence, you can interpret the info to make yourself a better fisherman. Try different colors and different types of plastic bodies to increase your crappie catches as water and weather conditions change......you'll be glad you did!

Boats

Chapter VI

Until the 60s, crappie fishermen rarely owned their own boats. Oh, sure, they fished out of boats but it was always one rented from a marina or fishing camp. They did own motors—usually a 5-horsepower, and some daredevils had an 18!

Boat liveries normally had 200 to 300 boats in inventory and you had to be there before daylight to get one on a spring weekend! The hustle and bustle of hundreds of frantic fishermen loading boats and trying to get to their favorite spot was chaotic but enjoyable.

Today those same boat liveries might have as few as six boats to rent! Crappie fishermen, perhaps the ones that were getting to the lake late on spring weekends, began buying their own boats. Momentum picked up to the point that most crappie fishermen either bought a boat or had their fishing partner buy one. Boat rentals suffered and fishing camp operators shifted into charging for launching to supplement lost revenue.

The boats being bought were the same types being rented, flat-bottom jon boats favored in the lowlands or deep V-bottoms favored by highlanders for big, open waters. Most were customized by the owners to suit their particular style of crappie fishing. Trolling motors weren't popular; at least in the South where a short sculling paddle was used from the front of the boat. A veteran angler skilled in the use of this paddle could maneuver a jon boat through the thickest tangles of willows and flooded backwaters while approaching spawning crappie with a stealth not possible with an electric trolling motor.

For sneaking up on spooky, shallow water crappie, the jon boat and a sculling paddle are unbeatable.

Photo courtesy of B&M Pole Co.

Sound travels too fast in the water and the silent swirl of a paddle is more effective for stalking spooky crappie. Sculling is still commonly practiced by a band of devotees who could afford the best of trolling motors if they so desired. They don't!

However, sculling has one drawback......it requires sitting in one spot all day and it takes a toll on the shoulders, back, and legs, especially if you're over 40 in age and waistline! The need for comfort increases proportionally with these two conditions!

Fortunately, we can now have the comfort we need in boats, designed with that purpose in mind. Unfortunately, we owe it all to the bass fishing industry triggered by bass tournaments and the development of fiberglass for boat hulls. First came wood, then aluminum, and finally fiberglass. Aluminum, however, has made a comeback in recent years as comfort features have been built in while retaining the ruggedness that made it popular. As Bob Holmes said when asked why he still fished out of his Alumnacraft, "Can you imagine bustin' through a willow brake with one of those high gloss metal flake hulls? I can't either!"

Boat manufacturers sprang up everywhere to answer the demands of the bass fishermen who wanted more speed, larger boats, better livewells, electronic equipment, lighter and stronger hulls. As some of the larger companies changed their hull designs seeking more speed, smaller operators bought their old hulls and continued to produce them under a different name. Tennessee became, and has remained, a leader in the manufacture of fishing vessels.

Crappie fishermen didn't need all of this pomp and circumstance; they preferred a boat with less frills and more function. Long runs weren't necessary so an aerodynamic hull wasn't important. RPMs mattered only in how slow and how long you could troll and not foul out the spark plugs. Aerated livewells were nice but an ice box was just as good because no fish were going to be released. The overriding feature was comfort......the ability to walk around in the boat and stretch tightening muscles. Here, the bass boat could provide a real service to the crappie fisherman!

In the mid-80s, boat manufacturers began to realize that a lot of their boats were being bought by crappie fishermen. It was a late blooming realization if ever there was one! Creel surveys by state game and fish agencies had documented for years that the overwhelming majority of anglers were after crappie! Plus, a big percentage of the bassing fraternity returned to crappie fishing when they remembered how much fun it was and how much better crappie fillets tasted. You could at least keep and eat crappie!

Of course, not all of the boat makers made this mistake—the old aluminum lines were still being put out by **POLAR KRAFT, ALUMNACRAFT, BASS PRO SHOPS, STARCRAFT, BUDDY, FISHER MARINE, MONARK** and a few others. Custom models were designed with carpeting, raised platforms, pedestal seats, dry storage, and livewells.

Aluminum, which had spelled doom for wooden boats, would not suffer the same fate from fiberglass. It remains popular today among serious crappie fishermen although many do prefer fiberglass models because of their larger size and seaworthiness.

For those preferring fiberglass, there are now gleaming, color-coordinated machines built specifically for the crappie fisherman by **PROCRAFT, FIBER-KING** and **RANGER.**

Here's a look at some of the available options in aluminum and fiberglass:

FISHER MARINE

Fisher Marine (P.O. Box 1256, West Point, Mississippi 39773) is in the forefront of aluminum fishing boat design and development. Their **GREY THUNDER CRAPPIE SERIES** has been custom designed by professional crappie fishermen. The charcoal grey exterior with red racing stripes appears to be fiberglass at first glance but it's 99 $\frac{9}{10}$ high-grade marine aluminum.

Two models, an 18-footer and a 16-footer, have standard features such as pedestal fishing chairs, wood-grained console, livewells, minnow wells, 12/24 volt wiring, rod holders, side rails, and a modified wave-tamer hull. That's not all the standard features but they're enough to let you know that it's a heckuva crappie rig!

Two other models with the same hull design but without the luxury additions are the **NETTER 16 DLX** and the **FISHER 15**. Both are carpeted with two fishing chairs, livewells, storage compartment, and trolling-motor stand with plug-in. Rated for less than 40HP, each is driven from the stern.

Other Fisher models for crappie fishermen include a number of flat-bottom jon boats and a V-bottom line they call their **SKIFF** series.

Fisher Marine's "Grey Thunder"

STARCRAFT

STARCRAFT (536 Michigan St., Topeka, Indiana 46571 (219) 593-2550) has been making boats since the 1920s and they know what they are doing. Their total lineup includes 84 models of fiberglass and aluminum, and the acquisition of the great Delhi factory is a definite feather in their cap. I was never able to wear out a Delhi jon boat I acquired in the early 60s, then sold during the bass boat craze and now wish I had back.

Starcraft offers 11 sizes of jon boats (10 to 16 feet) and any of the 11 could accommodate crappie fishermen but two models have been customized for that comfort we seem to crave—the **2048-16 DELUXE** which is carpeted, has console steering, a wet-well, dry storage and is rated for 40HP. The **1942-15 DELUXE** has marine grade carpeting on a raised aluminum floor with two storage seats and a flat bow surface for attaching a trolling motor. Starcraft's numbering system describes the dimensions of the boat: the first two numbers signify the height of the sides; the second two digits the width of the bottom; and the last two reveal the length.

Other models of interest to the crappie enthusiast include: the **SEA-FARER 16 DELUXE**, a modified V-hull for tackling big reservoirs; the **PIKEMASTER 160** which is supposedly designed for walleye fishing but it can be put to better use by crappie fishermen; and the **FISHMASTER 160**, another deep V, high-sided boat for open waters. The 160 has plenty of open floor space, vertical rod holders, aerated livewell, casting deck, dry storage and a steering console located nearer the bow than most others. It's rated for 90 horses.

Starcraft's Pikemaster 160 is a 16-footer that's big enough for reservoirs, yet small enough to handle tight spots in the timber and backwaters. It has an aerated livewell and trolling motor plug, plus several storage areas.

FIBERKING

FIBERKING INC. (100 G Street, Smyrna, TN 37167 (615) 459-4270) has been making fiberglass boats since 1969 in their plant near Nashville. In 1986, they added another model to their line—a crappie boat that was designed by two brothers in Murray, Kentucky.

Gary and Shane Darnell found a boat hull, after much experimentation, that could be customized to fit their crappie fishing needs. The boat was Fiberking's **BOMBER** bass boat which had a wide bow, a recessed casting deck and a deep V-hull.

The Darnells needed a craft seaworthy enough to handle the expanses of their home Kentucky Lake and other big reservoirs where crappie tournaments were being held. The boat's bow had to be broad enough to allow two fishermen to fish more than one pole side by side.

With the help of Buddy Boyd, Gary and Shane made the first prototypes which became so successful around Kentucky Lake that Fiberking began producing a **CRAPPIEMATE SERIES** that is beginning to attract the attention of tournament fishermen in other states.

The addition of a wooden bar with pole holders across the bow and a depth finder with the transducer mounted on the trolling motor makes it ideal for following a breakline, spider rig fishing or trolling. For more information about the **"DARNELL CRAPPIE MACHINE,"** contact: **Darnell Marine**, Rt. 3 Highway 94, Murray, KY 42071 (502) 753-3734.

The interior of a "**DARNELL CRAPPIE MACHINE**" shows a wide, recessed bow, a convenient livewell, foot-control trolling motor, and a row of 8 rod holders. A depth finder will either be added to the wooden bar in the middle of the rod holders or to the bow for constant viewing.

Note the three seat bases......two fishermen can fish side-by-side with plenty of elbow room or a lone fisherman can sit in the middle or on whichever side he wants to fish on. This type of seating arrangement allows equal opportunity for both anglers and is a definite factor in the amount of fish caught.

Rigged as shown in the picture, this "machine" is ready for spider-rig fishing. This boat is popular with crappie tournament contestants on strange lakes. Remove the bar and the boat becomes suitable for casting or tightlining a dropoff.

LOWE

LOWE INDUSTRIES (P.O. Box 989, Lebanon, Missouri 65536 (417) 532-9101) was selected to produce Crappiethon U.S.A.'s official boat. Lowe developed a 16-foot aluminum jon boat with a 72-inch beam, 48-inch bottom, a 7-degree V-hull, a flat aluminum double floor from front to back with carpet, two pedestal fishing seats, lockable storage, and a livewell. The two given away to the winners of the '88 Crappiethon Classic in Chattanooga, TN were really sharp.

Like Starcraft, **LOWE** offers an infinite variety of options to choose from in their semi-V and jon boat series. Semi-V models such as the **LUNKER II AND LUNKER III**, both 16-footers, have all the features for comfortable crappie fishing. A Limited Edition Package of features adds even more niceties. Lowe manufactures 30 different jon boats and has built and sold more than any other manufacturer. I particularly like their **HUSKY JON** which is available in 16-, 18-, or 10-foot lengths. The layout is basic simplicity with a wide casting deck and open space back to two split-seat platforms. The seat platforms are a natural for a bucket seat on one side and a depth finder on the other. Another fisherman would have to sit on a cooler or portable seat. For my needs, the cross braced bottom should be covered with a marine plywood floor and a removeable pedestal seat should be mounted on the casting deck.

All additions to the Husky Jon (24-inch sides, 60-inch bottom, 20-inch transom—an 18-footer weighing 440 lbs.) should be in an olive drab color because it doubles beautifully for duck and goose hunting! No, I don't crappie fish during waterfowl season unless they start breaking water around the blind!

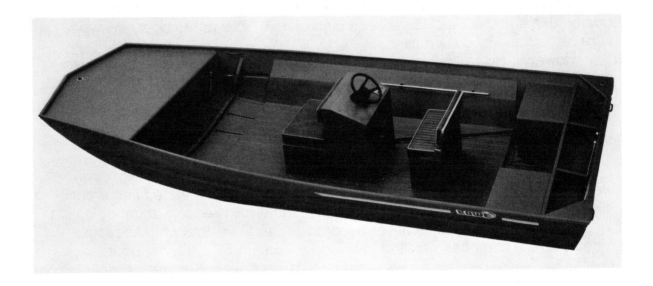

HUSKY JON MVB

POLAR KRAFT

POLAR KRAFT (9470 Lamar Ave., Olive Branch, MS 38654 (601) 895-5576) has been making aluminum jon boats for as long as I can remember and I don't think you can wear one out! The patented FLEX RIB allows the ribs of the boat to flex, thereby absorbing the shock of waves, logs and stumps rather than cracking the rib or welded joint.

Their standard square-ended jon boat has probably accounted for more crappie in the South than any other craft. The gauge of the aluminum is a hearty .072 and the Flex Ribs extend high on the sides of the boat, always a sure sign of quality construction.

However, Polar Kraft isn't resting on its laurels because the industry is changing fast and this Mississippi company is setting new standards while maintaining the quality that's been their trademark for years.

To meet the increased demands of today's crappie fisherman, Polar Kraft has introduced three new models—a 14-footer and two 16-foot models complete with all the optional equipment you'll ever need.

They also offer a Modified V-hull in 14- to 18-foot lengths for big, open water situations and a Mallard series is designed to be converted into a duck blind for those who don't crappie fish during waterfowl season; a dandy option.

Some particularly innovative research at the Olive Branch, Mississippi manufacturing plant has resulted in the development of a "Tunnel Boat." A beefed up tunnel has been engineered into a jon boat hull at the transom which allows it to maneuver in as little as 10 inches of water......an important consideration in spring time crappie fishing. Polar Kraft calls it the "TOP WATER TUNNEL."

Another exciting piece of research also involves the "Tunnel Boat" and it consists of attaching Yamaha's Jet Drive outboard to the transom to add even greater shallow water capability.

With the "Jet Drive" and the "Tunnel," a fisherman may be able to navigate across a heavy dew! If this combination works, I hope to be one of the first to put it in the water!

Boats

Flex Rib™ Tough. Allows ribs to flex, absorbing shock of wave action rather than cracking the rib or welded joint.

MV-1751T

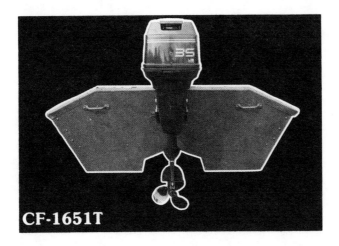

CF-1651T

PROCRAFT

PROCRAFT (P.O. Box 720, Murfreesboro, TN 37133 (615) 890-1593) is another fiberglass boat manufacturer that has made the switch to the booming crappie fishing market. They produce two different lengths (15-foot and 16-foot) in fiberglass which have a wide front deck for side-by-side fishing. The broad bow is reminiscent of the original Astroglass hull, one of the first to enter the fiberglass market in the late 60s and perhaps the most popular design to ever hit the water.

The 15-footer is particularly attractive for its ease of handling without sacrificing safety and roominess; plus, it has the advantage of gas economy.

Both models have a long list of standard features and they are detail-finished in a manner that's made **PROCRAFT** renown in the business.

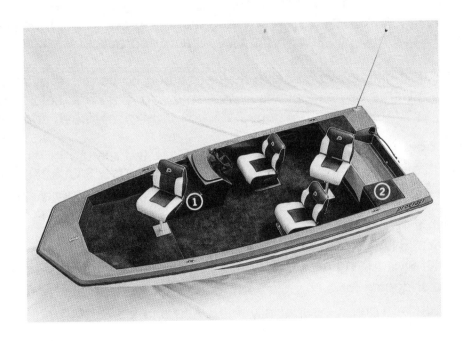

Procraft's Crappie Model

PONTOONS

Don't overlook a pontoon boat as the ultimate crappie fishing rig. A lot of people haven't. It also serves as a great family fun package and is indeed the best of both worlds.

At first thought, you might assume that pontoon boats would be very limited in the year-round pursuit of crappie. Actually, the opposite is true. Properly rigged with pedestal seats on the bow, rod holders, trolling motor and depth finder, a pontoon boat can pursue crappie wherever they go with the exception of thick timber in the spring. And even then, fishing need not stop because not all of the fish will be in the timber at the same time.

After the spawn, pontoons really come into their own when crappie are scattered and trolling is the ideal way to pick up a limit. In rivers, oxbows, natural lakes and reservoirs, pontoon boat trolling is the best method throughout the summer and early fall. It's also the most practical type of boat for fishing under the lights at night.

On lowland lakes where meandering creek and river channels harbor concentrations of crappie, the pontoon boat is ideal for following the breakline if the transducer is properly rigged on the trolling motor. Two anglers can work the edge of the drop by casting jigs or tightlining with minnows while two more can fish off the sides with minnows. As a guide, I always wanted a pontoon boat so that I could take out four or five paying customers instead of two!

And talk about comfort! Pontoons are the "Max!" There's plenty of walking around or lying down room with facilities for cooking (grills) and eating (dining table). Their only drawback is trailering and launching but this can be overcome with practice and you should practice, practice, practice! Or else rent a boatslip at the local marina.

A number of different companies make pontoon boats and they're all fairly basic in design with a few exceptions. Choose a floor plan and color scheme that's right for you and take the plunge, which is very reasonable, and they hold their value.

BASS PRO SHOPS offers a model ideally suited for the crappie angler whose only drawback is its name......**"BASS BUGGY!"** **STARCRAFT, LOWE, POLAR KRAFT** and several others also produce a quality craft.

Lowe Industries manufactures a **FISH N FUN** (well named) pontoon complete with fishing seats, livewell and trolling motor socket.

Starcraft's **STARDECK 200 FISHERMAN** has fisherman extras such as a trolling motor site, fishing seats, rod racks, and a center mounted console.

If you're shopping for a crappie craft, don't look too long at a pontoon boat or you'll end up with one......especially if the wife and kids are along! Or your neighbor!

Equipped with a bow-mounted trolling motor, fishing chairs, and a depth locator, the pontoon boat is simply the most comfortable boat of all in which to pursue crappie. Realizing the importance of this market, companies such as Starcraft, Lowe, Bass Pro Shops and Polar Kraft are offering added conveniences in the form of aerated livewells, rod storage, rod racks, center consoles, and trolling motor plug-ins.

Lowe Sunbird Fish N Fun

PONTOON TRANSDUCER INSTALLATION

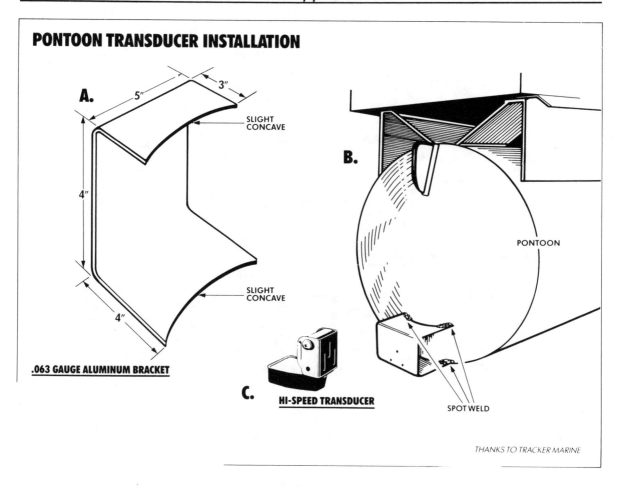

A.

5"

3"

SLIGHT
CONCAVE

4"

SLIGHT
CONCAVE

4"

.063 GAUGE ALUMINUM BRACKET

B.

PONTOON

C.

HI-SPEED TRANSDUCER

SPOT WELD

THANKS TO TRACKER MARINE

Pontoon boats have proven to be excellent crappie fishing machines but they present one problem—the installation of the transducer.

Most pontoons have slightly convex design but they do vary and will require some modification.

Take a small sheet of .063 gauge aluminum, 5 inches wide by 11 inches long. Bend the aluminum sheet as shown in illustration A. Depending upon the configuration of the pontoon, grind the edges to fit the contour if necessary.

The bracket is then spot welded to the pontoon as shown in illustration B. This should only be done by someone familiar with aluminum welds.

It is also very important that the bottom of the bracket be flush with the bottom of the pontoon to assure a smooth flow of water between the two.

A high speed transducer can now be installed on the bracket after drilling the necessary holes required by the transducer. Check the detailed instructions provided by the transducer manufacturer to insure a proper reading.

REELFOOT BOAT

One other boat deserves special mention because it is an interesting piece of American folklore. It is neither aluminum or fiberglass and it is unique to the northwest corner of Tennessee, although it could also be used on any waters where stumps are a constant threat. Aptly termed a "stump jumper" by the residents of Reelfoot Lake, outsiders refer to it as a "**REELFOOT BOAT.**"

Necessity being the Mother of Invention, the fishermen, hunters, and trappers traversing the stump-filled environs of the "Earthquake Lake" had to have a craft that could take the constant battering of underwater hazards and be able to get off a stump when "high centered!" The result was, and still is, a hand-made wooden (cypress) boat 10 feet long, pointed on both ends with two seats on the floor and powered by a small (one-two hp) gas engine which sits in the middle of the boat between the seats! A metal plate on the bottom protects the propeller and allows it to slide over stump after stump. On Reelfoot, you're never far from a stump!

Without the motor, the Reelfoot boat is similar to a Louisiana pirogue and may owe its existence to that region because Reelfoot is typical Louisiana bayou country seemingly out of place as far north as Tennessee!

Reelfoot boats are still being made on a limited basis near the lake. For more information, contact: Reelfoot Lake State Park, Rt. 1, Tiptonville, TN 38079 (901) 253-7756.

The "Reelfoot Boat" was developed to navigate the stumpfields of Tennessee's Reelfoot Lake.

Winter

Chapter VII

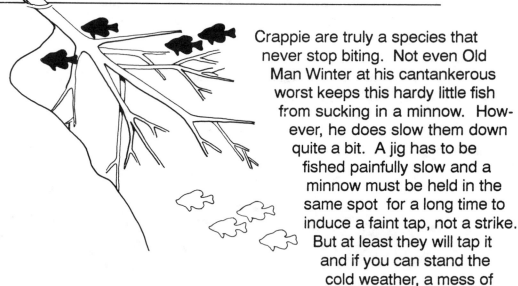

Crappie are truly a species that never stop biting. Not even Old Man Winter at his cantankerous worst keeps this hardy little fish from sucking in a minnow. However, he does slow them down quite a bit. A jig has to be fished painfully slow and a minnow must be held in the same spot for a long time to induce a faint tap, not a strike. But at least they will tap it and if you can stand the cold weather, a mess of fillets will be the reward. There are several systems that work depending on your latitude. In the northern states, fishing through ice is the only alternative unless there's a steam plant handy. Veteran ice fishermen begin their preparation long before it gets cold. They'll spend a few hours on the lake triangulating objects on the shoreline that zeroes them in on a favorite dropoff or deep water structure that holds crappie. The method is simple but it has to be precise and it has to be accurately noted on a detailed map. Being close doesn't count in winter crappie fishing. The school is tight on the structure and they may stay there all winter. Employ a depth finder to insure that you're where you ought to be to make contact. Scrape the snow off of the ice and use a little anti-freeze to set the transducer on in order to get a reliable reading. Keep moving the transducer until you're satisfied with the location. It's easier to move the transducer than it is to drill holes in the ice!

Small minnows are probably more productive than jigs in ice fishing. I think that this is also true throughout the rest of the country in the dead of winter. I'm sure there are those who disagree and they'd be right, too. At least be prepared to try both because some days a crappie will not hit a minnow when they will hit a jig and vice versa.

Fish with a small minnow hooked through the back or a small ($1/32$- or $1/64$-ounce) marabou jig on ultralight line. Lakes and rivers are extremely clear in winter—clearer than at any other time of the year due to the lack of sediment, plankton, and other organisms. Water clarity thus dictates the use of a fine diameter line in the two-pound to four-pound class. Try a minnow and a jig in the same ice hole and experiment with them long enough to draw a conclusion. Add more factors to the experiment—spray one bait or lure with Fish Formula and see if it makes a difference. I mean, you've got to come up with something constuctive while gazing at a hole in the ice all day long.

Moving southward out of the polar regions, somewhere near the Mason/Dixon line or the Ohio River, we find that the big reservoirs don't freeze over in normal winters. In abnormal winters they do. Impoundments in Virginia, Kentucky, Tennessee, North Carolina, and Arkansas usually have their coves and bays covered with a thin sheet of ice but the main lake will be ice free.

The edge of the ice, where the cove or bay encounters open water, is the place to fish in the winter......especially in deep, clear highland-type lakes such as Douglas in East Tennessee. Walter Green of Swan Creek Dock breaks through the ice in the cove out to its mouth where he casts randomly along the edge with jigs and ultralight equipment. The crappie "suspend" in open water and usually not very deep. Exploring the various depths with a count-down method and a little patience invariably leads him to the location of the school and a stringer of crappie. Trolling the edge of the ice might also work if you could troll slow enough. Drifting with the wind would be better. Drifters and trollers should put out several poles rigged at different depths until a fish is caught and the proper depth is determined. The holding depth, however, won't remain the same and will vary as the amount of light penetration changes during the day. When you realize that you haven't had a strike in a while, they've changed depths and you're probably fishing under them because, more than likely, the school has moved shallower. Movements this time of year tend to be vertical rather than horizontal.

Douglas Lake is a typical highland impoundment and this technique should work on any other highland lake during the winter when the coves, creeks, and bays freeze but not the main body. Be sure not to break ice with a fiberglass hull, it will ruin a gel-coat finish very quickly. A good aluminum boat with ice runners is recommended for this kind of operation. Ice runners also add strength to the hull for other rough uses such as running across log jams, beaver dams, and sand bars.

On lakes which have not iced over because of the relative mildness of the weather, there's an excellent way to catch crappie that's the favorite of many and can be practiced on any reservoir with active tributaries. The tributaries are the place. Seek them out even if it means going to the headwaters of the lake to find the proper situation. On lowland lakes, it won't be a problem to find a productive tributary; natural lakes won't have many, if any, and midland lakes such as Percy Priest near Nashville, Tennessee have their finest winter crappie angling primarily in creeks in the upper reaches of the impoundment. Priest is drawn down in the winter to 10,000 acres from its normal 14,000 of late spring and summer. All man-made lakes are drawn down for the sake of flood control. As a midland lake and relatively young (impounded 1966), Priest's tributaries are well defined and still have sharp dropoffs with stumps and planted brushpiles along the edges. Most of the timber was removed prior to impoundment.

Crappie are found in all of the creeks that have a continuous source of water but they won't be found in the winter in the upper ends of the creek (unless there's a warm spring). They prefer to stay near the main body of the lake......at least within 500 yards depending on the size of the lake and the size of the tributary. A reliable rule of thumb is that they'll be concentrated in the first one-third of the creek as you enter it from the lake. Usually the junction of the creek and river channel is as good a holding spot as there is and it's the perfect place to start fishing if the water's not too deep.

Turn on the flasher, graph or LCR and begin outlining the creek channel dropoffs. Drop a marker at the first suspicious blips on the electronic unit and then drop another marker 20 or 30 yards further up the creek. Anchor between the two markers close enough to the first marker to make a leisurely cast beyond the school and retrieve it through them at the exact depth they're holding. Preciseness is important. The school is tightly bunched and they're not going to chase a bait.

Anchoring is vital to the success of this misson. Two anchors are essential and can be of any material, store-bought, or homemade. Wind, of course, will necessitate heavier weights. Position the boat perpendicular to the dropoff with the bow extending a few feet over shallower water. Drop the first anchor and pay out enough line to allow the boat handler to swing the rear of the boat perpendicular to the dropoff where he releases his anchor. This way, everybody has an equal chance of properly presenting his jig to the hotspot! When the action stops, up anchors and outline another stretch of creek channel. Keep in mind that the school may have either moved up onto the adjacent flat as the sun got warmer or gone deeper into the creek channel if there's been a lot of boat traffic.

Another method to catch fish here is with minnows on the Kentucky Lake tightline rig. This rig has a one-ounce bell sinker on the bottom of the line and one, two or three hooks tied off at intervals above the sinker. It's a great dropoff prober. Outline the dropoff as before only space your markers farther apart and use extra markers to indicate an irregularity such as a ditch, projection, or pocket. Work into the wind and simply cross-stitch the edge of the dropoff with the tightline rig until a gathering is located. Either anchor very carefully at that point or stay on top of them with the trolling motor. (There's no better way to spend a winter day!)

With the proper clothing, winter crappie fishing can be comfortable and productive.

However, there are other ways, depending on the particular watercourse and its idiosyncrasies. For example, the Tennessee/Tombigbee waterway is a new chain of lakes creating the long-awaited link to the Gulf of Mexico from the Tennessee River. This chain of lakes is lowland in nature with the exception of the northern-most reservoir called Bay Springs. An in-depth description of the waterway is included in Chapter XVIII (Best Crappie Waters) but here I want to discuss a wintertime situation that Ronnie Guyton of Columbus, Mississippi reported to me. Ronnie is one of the premier crappie fishermen in the South.

Even the best of crappie fishermen needs a little luck in order to locate or relocate a school of crappie. Some profess to rather having luck than skill but I'll take skill and preparation and create "luck." Ronnie is the same way. For the better part of an early December day, he hadn't been able to raise any fish out of his usually productive fall haunts. He decided that they had to be in deep water so he began looking in the deep holes of a major tributary in open water. Why there? Just a feeling that the good ones get sometimes.

Ronnie dropped a tube jig over the side into 35 feet of water but it never made the bottom. A slab crappie nailed the jig about 10 feet down! And then another! And another! Until Ronnie had caught his legal limit. Not all of them came from the 10-foot depth. He caught them at all depths down to the bottom. The bigger fish seemed to be nearer the bottom; a pattern that was to hold throughout December and into January when storm systems and muddy water dispersed the fish. Before Mother Nature came to their rescue, Ronnie estimates that over 10,000 fish were caught during that time period in a deep water spot about the size of a football field! Wow! What a honey hole! It's the stuff crappie dreams are made of!

Crappie were literally stacked like cordwood for fishermen who caught them equally well on minnows and jigs with any kind of tackle.

A similar set-up exists in the bigger, natural lakes of Florida, especially Okeechobee. Results may not be as quick or as staggering as the previous example, but catches of over a 100 a day are obtainable if you know what to do. And it's simple. Forget about bass and the grassbeds and concentrate on the deepest open water you can find. Deep in Okeechobee means less than 18 feet! Put out as many poles as can be comfortably fished and start drifting over the clean, sandy bottom. Minnows are preferred but jigs will work. Keep the offerings near the bottom and you'll be in fish before drifting too far. On calm days, use the electric trolling motor to stay in motion and give lift and life to the bait.

Crappie addicts in more northern climes would be well advised to start the season in sunny Florida weeks before the local crappie start hitting.

Winter crappie fishing has tradiitonally been thought of in terms of probing deep water structures as the only way to take home a mess of fillets. However, this is one of those axioms that's not always true (in crappie fishing, I don't think there are any absolute axioms). It may not happen in all crappie waters but they will move into water less than three feet deep for extended periods of time in mid-winter! This practice is not generally well known because the few

Fishing A Dropoff

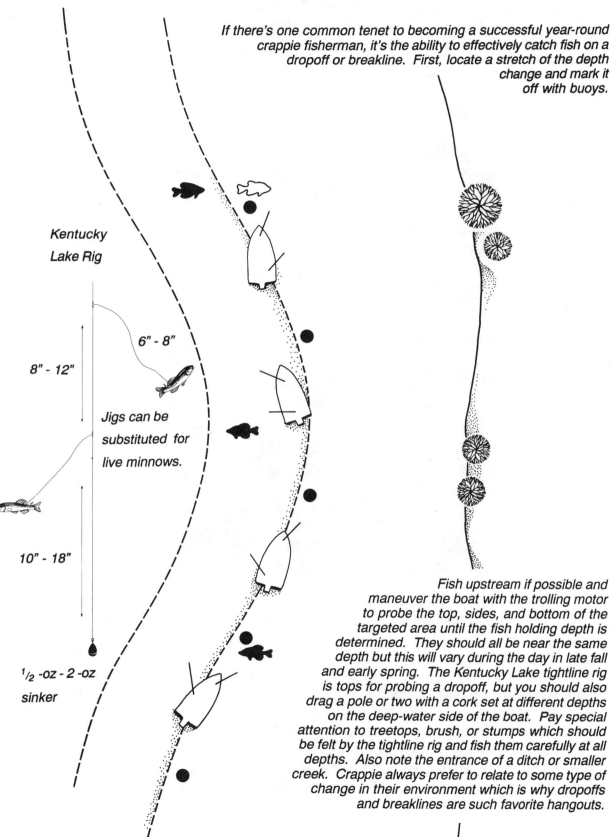

If there's one common tenet to becoming a successful year-round crappie fisherman, it's the ability to effectively catch fish on a dropoff or breakline. First, locate a stretch of the depth change and mark it off with buoys.

Kentucky
Lake Rig

6" - 8"

8" - 12"

Jigs can be substituted for live minnows.

10" - 18"

$^1/_2$ -oz - 2 -oz
sinker

Fish upstream if possible and maneuver the boat with the trolling motor to probe the top, sides, and bottom of the targeted area until the fish holding depth is determined. They should all be near the same depth but this will vary during the day in late fall and early spring. The Kentucky Lake tightline rig is tops for probing a dropoff, but you should also drag a pole or two with a cork set at different depths on the deep-water side of the boat. Pay special attention to treetops, brush, or stumps which should be felt by the tightline rig and fish them carefully at all depths. Also note the entrance of a ditch or smaller creek. Crappie always prefer to relate to some type of change in their environment which is why dropoffs and breaklines are such favorite hangouts.

fishermen who are out just don't assume that any fish would be shallow in cold weather. But they often are and I believe the reason is the presence of baitfish—food. Crappie, even though their metabolism is slowed by cold water temperatures, still forage for minnows in winter.

Wintertime crappie fishing requires ultra-light equipment and the ability to pinpoint a school of fish.

Two examples will help prove my point. Three of us were duck hunting in mid-January in some flooded river bottoms in southeast Arkansas. Hunting had been exceptionally good because the Mississippi River had overflowed its banks into adjacent pin oak flats where mallards could feed on a bounty of acorns. But the river had crested and had been falling for several days. When the water left the bottoms, so did the ducks. However, our loss was the local commercial fishermen's gain, who were having a field day with their barrel nets set in the runouts where the overflow was falling back to the main sloughs and channels!

Being curious by nature, it's always interesting to pull up a net to see what's been caught—if, and only if, you know whose net it is and he happens to be a very good friend. Otherwise, the practice is not recommended. The same is true of a trotline.

Anyway, one net we looked into was loaded with crappie and since it was illegal to take gamefish in nets, we helped release them......all except a few that I kept for scientific study! Not only were these fish lively and vigorous, they were fat as mud and had bulging stomachs. When I opened the stomachs to examine the contents (scientific research is a dirty business), they were full of minnows in partial stages of digestion! These crappie were actively feeding in water less than six-feet deep in the middle of January!

The other example involved a simple observation of nature. One cold February day I was driving along the shoreline of Wheeler Lake, a lowland

Stake beds are normally put in during the winter drawdown in areas that will have three to six feet of water over them when the reservoir rises in the spring. Marking a nearby tree with spray paint can help locate the bed.

impoundment of the Tennessee River near Decatur, Alabama. Wheeler is noted for its stump fields which become more evident during the winter draw-down. Water depth around the exposed stumps varies from six inches to three feet. Again, ducks were the reason I was out there and even though the season was over; I hoped to get some photographs of the different species in flight. There weren't many ducks but the stumpfields were crawling with Great Blue Herons! It looked like a full blown convention of wading birds perched on the stumps staring intently into the water.

I knew what they were looking for and I wondered if crappie could also be looking for the same thing. A few hours later I had the answer—yes, crappie were in the stumpfields and they would take a tube jig fished ever so slowly under a sliding cork! Great Blue Herons know their fishing!

A similar situation with a slightly different technique exists in the numerous oxbows and bendways of the Mississippi River from St. Louis to New Orleans. Crappie fishermen find shallow stumps and willows where they either use a lively minnow and a small cork or a $1/16$- or $1/32$-ounce jig on a 10- to 14-foot pole. Minnows are hard to beat for winter crappie fishing. Their only drawback is getting your hands wet while baiting the hook. It can't be helped because Wells Lamont has not invented a glove to hold a live minnow while sticking steel under his dorsal fin. The best compromise other than a charcoal bucket or portable heater, is a pair of gloves with the thumb and first two fingers cut off at the first joint. Leave the other two fingers intact.

Gloves are important and so is the rest of a winter fisherman's wardrobe. Proper clothing is absolutely essential for enjoying a day's fishing, not to mention survival.

Layering is the term universally applied to winter clothing but piling on layers of clothes is self-defeating and self limiting. It really only takes four or five layers of the right garments to comfortably withstand the coldest weather. My personal selection starts with a heavy-weight suit of polypropylene underwear, topped with a cotton turtleneck, a wool shirt, and wool trousers. The last layer is a goose down outfit of overalls and a jacket. Some prefer a one piece coverall which is excellent. Flotation coats can, and probably should, substitute for the down jacket for safety's sake and they'll keep you almost as warm.

Choose a pair of felt-lined rubber-bottom, leather-top boots at least one whole size larger than your regular shoe size. The $1/4$-inch felt liner is the crucial ingredient along with a little air space. Air space is also vital in the layers of clothes and going up another size in outer garments is essential to warmth. For raingear, the size differential is even greater and should be two or three sizes larger than normal.

Body heat escapes quickly if the head is left uncovered and it should never be in winter crappie fishing. Use a motorcycle helmet with a clear plastic visor for running the boat to different spots. Then don a ski mask while fishing. The ski mask is the one item that I absolutely won't go to the lake without.

Individual preferences of layering will naturally vary depending on personality and body chemistry but the basic theme should be adhered to for comfortable fishing. Comfortable may not be a good word because some body part (usually the hands) is always going to be cold! Tolerable may be a better word.

STEAM PLANT CRAPPIE

Steam plants such as this one on Old Hickory Lake near Gallatin, Tennessee provide excellent fishing for crappie. Warm water is discharged into a canal or channel which flows into the cooler waters of a river or reservoir. Because the discharge is so much warmer (10 to 30 degrees) both forage species and game fish seek out this comfort zone. Threadfin and Gizzard shad are especially attracted to this new-found warmth because they tend to die when water temperatures drop below 45 degrees. Crappie react both to the warmth and to the presence of shad.

Crappie rarely venture into the boils and swift currents created at the generator site. They prefer to get out of the force of the current by lying behind obstructions such as wing walls, rock piles, and pilings......or in the eddy where the current changes. Other potential crappie locations include any break along the channel in the form of a treetop, gravel bar or a small creek intersection.

Crappie are also subject to "suspending" in a bend of the channel anywhere along its route to the river as well as the junction of the river itself. Points of land and riprapped points along this route can also hold concentrations of fish.

Casting the banks with jigs and trolling are the preferred methods although fishing from shore can be just as effective, if not more so.

Because of the relatively confined water surface offered by a steam plant, it doesn't take many fishermen to get in each other's way. If you can't fish during the week and have to fish on weekends, try it at night! Crappie are notorious nocturnal ramblers in steam plant discharges!

Guides are Cheap......A Bargain

Chapter VIII

Guides aren't cheap but they are a bargain. Think back for a moment to the last time you visited a doctor's, dentist's or lawyer's office. Chances are that the time actually spent under their care could be measured in minutes and you're still getting monthly statements a year later! Don't even contemplate what the bill might have been had you received their attention for eight hours.

I once had the bright idea that I would swap a guided fishing trip or trips for an equitable amount of time spent with my friendly dentist in his chair. Bartering was the "in" thing. However, when I figured out how much time I would have to spend with him, there were only a few days left in August that I could pursue my guiding career! I know, you're paying for expertise and skill developed from formal education and finally through experience at your expense (financial and physical).

Consider some basic facts about education: a 40 year-old lawyer, dentist or doctor will have a four year college education and three years of advanced schooling. Doctors who specialize will have an additional three to four years of training. Under normal processes, the doctor or lawyer will graduate from college at 21, from graduate school at 24 and have 16 years of experience at the age of 40.

A fishing guide, on the other hand, a true professional in every sense of the word, may also have a college degree. More than likely, he won't have an advanced degree but he has been studying his fishing craft since the ripe old age of eight! Which gives the same age man 32 years of experience versus 16 years in the other professional brackets. Double!

So why do most people think that it's outrageous for a guide to charge them $100 a day to go fishing!? Many of these same folks are charging their clients $100 an hour. And they're the ones who didn't specialize. A good crappie guide earns, and I mean literally earns, his $12.50 an hour for eight hours on the water. A few get as much as $15 an hour but many labor for as little as $75 a day.

The outboard motor mechanic who works on his motor after a few months of factory training demands $20 to $30 an hour! Economics continue to mount on the debit side of the guide's ledger; all of which boils down to, "Hire a guide; not because he needs the money, but because you need to catch some fish and the guide fee will be money well spent."

Practically all reputable crappie waters have one thing in common—they're big. When you cross the dams of Kentucky Lake, Bulls Shoals, Sardis, Eufala, and Wheeler, their expansive waters can be demoralizing to even experienced fishermen. Where in the world in these thousands of acres am I going to find fish? The local newspapers had been printing glowing reports and pictures of incredible catches being made by everybody that could find the water.

The quickest solution is what we've been talking about—hire a guide on the first day and then fish the same way on identical types of structures for the balance of your stay. Please don't go back to the guide's holes unless he says it's all right. He's probably worked hard putting in fish attractors and they are his sole source of income. Take what you've learned and apply it in similar circumstances. And there's nothing wrong with hiring a guide each day. Guides would rather book a 3-day-trip than 3 one-day trips with different people. The best guides have built their reputation over the years by accumulating a solid list of satisfied customers that return each spring during the peak spawning runs. During March, April, and May, reservations and deposits should be made weeks in advance.

Of course, the foibles of spring weather being what they are, your fishing trip may not coincide with the peak of the shallow water activity. Go ahead and go, honor your reservation unless the guide agrees that it's a waste of time at the present. Conscientious guides who want you to return next year will honestly advise you to put off the trip even though they'll lose that day's fee. Keeping you happy insures the word-of-mouth advertising that's the backbone of their business.

The flip side of the coin is your obligation to the guide. You have to be a good customer. Some of the rules and reasons are:

Rule #1—*Reservations.* Call and cancel your reservations if you can't make the trip; the sooner you can let a guide know that he won't see your smiling face on the day in question, the more time he'll have to pick up another party or at least have one morning off to go turkey hunting.

Rule #2—*Be ready.* Nothing is more aggravating for the guide than being all set and ready to go and nobody's showed up. You'd talked the night before

The author (left) and "Shorty" Groom of Nashville, Tennessee, one of the greatest fishermen of all time, with a stringer of fine crappie taken from Hurricane Creek on Lake Barkley. If you can't afford a guide, try to fish with someone who knows more about fishing than you do!

when you checked in the motel so he knows you're in the area. Overslept! Hangover! Ummm. The guide starts counting his time at the agreed upon 6 a.m. When the client finally arrives at 10:30 a.m., he's got 3 1/2 hours left on his eight hour fee! Result—everybody's mad. Harsh words are spoken and the day is ruined. Keep in mind, and most people simply don't, that a fishing guide is a qualified professional and his day in the office is the same as any other business man, 8 to 10 hours. I don't care how you have romanticized and perceived his job to be because all he does is fish for a living; a guide, your guide, is not going to be hanging around the marina waiting for you to decide when the time is right! Not unless you pay him enough! And then he can become an expert at hanging around marinas!

Rule #3—*Surprise Guests*. I once had a last minute guide trip booked through a marina for a father/son team. Splendid! Love to see the old man take his offspring on a fish excursion. Does wonders for them both and after diligent instruction, the father finally gets the hang of it while the youngster is filling the ice chest *muy pronto*. Anyway, I sped by boat from the marina to the resort where they were staying. As I pulled into the resort's dock, there was some sort of reunion or picnic going on. I thought I heard cries of "It's the guide!" "It's the guide!" Naw, just my imagination. Wrong. There were three father/son teams clamoring down the hill towards "the guide." After I became coherent again, the story unraveled. It seems that each year, this group of fathers takes their boys on a vacation to a site that the group preselects.

"Yes, yours is a noble cause but I'm going back and throttle that marina reservation agent!"

"No, No," I was assured, "We have rented two other boats. They'll just follow along and fish in the rear." Now if there's one thing that a guide doesn't like (other than this list of rule infractions), it's a follow boat. Usually there's a small charge for a follow boat of $25 to $50 which should be twice as much because it's such a pain to get the follow boat in position to catch fish. Guides hate 'em but have to go along to keep harmony in the group. The follow boat invariably has a smaller motor which requires slowing down and waiting for it to catch up. I have a 150 hp Mariner Magnum on one of the hulls that came out of the wind tunnel.

Two of the father/son teams were going to follow in 12' aluminum boats with 5 hp kickers! Surprisingly, the trip was one of the most enjoyable I had all season. The crappie were in shallow water around stumps and brushpiles on secondary points in the bays and coves. Low water levels were keeping them out of the shoreline bushes and they were readily accessible to small jigs and ultralight equipment. However, I failed with one of the fathers. I never did convince him to turn his borrowed spinning rod and reel right side up!

Rule #4—*How to fish.* Try to fish the way the guide suggests. Obviously, it's the guide's business and in the best interest of his livelihood to know how to catch crappie in his lake. Believe me, when you go to a strange lake, a good rule of thumb is to try to find out how the locals are catching fish and then follow suit. This goes for any kind of fish, fresh or saltwater. The guide is one of the locals. He knows, or is supposed to know, when the fish have left deep water and entered the creeks, how far up the creeks they've gone, and at what depth they are "suspending." In other words, he's keeping daily tabs on their movements which are extensive from February to June and again in the fall. In summer and winter months, movements are minimal but the schools are hard to pinpoint. Because he's in tune with these locations, he will also know what it takes to put fish in the boat! Remember, that's the reason for hiring him in the first place. If anyone was lucky enough to go to a new lake and immediately begin to decimate the species, that person shouldn't be on a lake, he should sell the family business and head for Las Vegas.

This rule is not inviolate, however; sometimes a fisherman can impart valuable fishing knowledge to a guide who would be a fool not to take heed. The same is true of a fisherman who doggedly sticks to his methods while others in the boat and adjacent boats are hauling in slabs. A middle ground can be reached with discussion and compromise. Let the guide know beforehand if you'd like to try casting jigs with ultralight tackle. Or that your arthritis won't permit casting at all and a pole and minnow is the only way you can effectively fish. A good guide will accommodate your needs and adjust his game plan even though it means a loss of face at the cleaning tables.

Rule #5—*Reimburse the guide for lost lures and damaged equipment.* Generally, if you're going to fish as the guide suggests, you're not going to have the type of tackle to match the conditions unless the guide has informed you prior to leaving home. Many guides prefer to furnish the equipment because it insures that you'll fish in the manner he directs. The key word in the previous statement is "furnishes," which means that he expects to get it back! A rod and reel or pole may be an instrument of idle pursuit to you, but to a guide, it's the tool of his trade just the same as the surgeon's scalpel, the plumber's pipe wrench, etc.... So if a guide's equipment is damaged or lost due to your actions, at least offer reimbursement. Most guides probably won't accept the offer, having already figured a certain loss of equipment for the season. Besides, they haven't given you their good stuff anyway; at least I wouldn't.

Loss of lures is also not important to guides who usually pour their own jigs and buy grub bodies in bulk. Even so, a day's fishing in crappie cover can result in the loss of a hundred jigs! It mounts up quickly. Again offer restitution. Or at least ask before the trip or the next day's fishing where the types of lure being used can be purchased. Jigs, as I said before, are usually no problem. A guide is set up to absorb that loss. Another little bait, however, that's becoming very popular because it's a crappie catching fool around shallow water brush is the roadrunner, or pony head jig with a small spinner and grub body. The addition of the spinner runs the cost of this lure up to a point that makes it prohibitively expensive to lose in quantities.

Crappie guides have the advantage in this respect (and all others) over their bassing guide counterparts who can ill afford to have a client lose four or five of today's high priced plugs without compensation.

Rule #6—*Bellyaching and Moaning.* O. K., it's going to happen. You've hired the best guide on the lake. Paid him top dollar. He's limited out for the past 10 straight days with other clients. You've arrived the day after a major storm-frontal system. Temperatures are dropping. With some hard, day-long fishing, 15 to 20 fish are brought to boat. Not bad under those conditions. Oh, you expected to be culling your limit by noon and have constantly berated the poor guide with bellyaches and moans. Did you take the weather into account? Fronts, the bane of all fishermen, drastically alter the habits of crappie. Those in shallow water migrate back to the first deep-water dropoff while others may move out of the creek to the main body of the lake.

When in this state of flux, they are extremely reluctant to bite. Their metabolism puts them off their feed for a couple of days. Only a relative few can be enticed into taking a jig or a minnow. Give the guide a break, he's no miracle worker. He's feeling worse than you are about the sudden change in weather but he'll know the post-front concentration areas where you can scratch out a few fish by going at it hard all day.

This is the number one reason why there aren't more fishing guides. I've asked a number of expert fishermen with time on their hands why they didn't do some guiding. They universally answer that they couldn't stand to take a client's money and not catch any fish. It's true......that's the hardest thing a guide has to do. But the fact of life is that any guide is going to have fishless days and he can't afford to forego his fee due to factors beyond his control. If a dentist pulls the wrong tooth, do you get your money back?

I've only known of one guide who would give an unfortunate client a free half-day of fishing at a later date if the trip was a total washout—Harold Morgan of Nashville, Tennessee, who guides on nearby Percy Priest Lake. However, Harold rarely ever has a washout so he doesn't have to give many free days. I've also heard of some guides who will take you out on a no fish—no pay basis. When you're good, you can offer the paying customer alternatives such as these, which, at the very least, inspire confidence.

Now that you understand that guides are human and that your success is necessary for their success, it's easy to see why moaning and groaning isn't going to effect any remedies. Unless, of course, your guide is asleep in the back of the boat after an all night drinking spree!

To be successful, a guide has to make sure that his clients catch fish, even if it means the day's catch will be less than it might have been due to the time spent on instruction. The qualities of teaching, patience and understanding are the cornerstone of an outstanding guide.

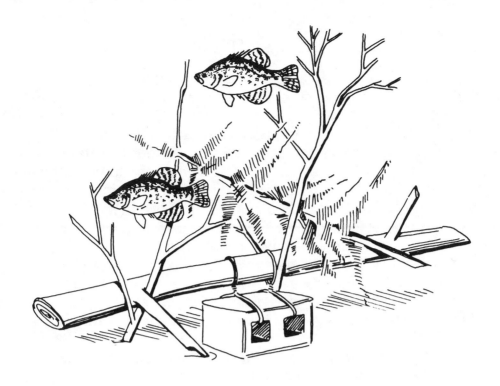

Fish Attractors

Chapter IX

If you were playing a word association game and the word "Crappie" came up, what would you say? Fish? Minnows? Jigs? Maybe, but I think a crappie fisherman should say brush, treetops, stumps, stake beds. Because when you say "crappie," you have to think of woody cover, at least for white crappie. Rarely will they be very far from some type and naturally there are exceptions. On most Florida and northern lakes, aquatic vegetation takes the place of woody species as cover and black crappie are predominant. But plant a brushpile or fish attractor in these waters and they'll flock to it like a new restaurant in town.

The great dam-building eras of the past 40 years produced hundreds of large reservoirs, most of which were cleared by bulldozers and the timber cut flush with the ground. This older scheme of things has been replaced in recent years by a timber removal pattern based on sound biological knowledge that is of greater value to the fishery resource and ultimately to the fisherman. Reservoirs in the 80s have, for the most part, left a certain percentage of timber standing in coves, creeks, and bays. The Tennessee/Tombigbee Waterway is a classic example. State and federal fishery biologists had the luxury of being able to design a fish management plan that would achieve optimum results without interfering with the waterway's priority objective of navigation. Entire coves and small creeks were left timbered, as were selected high spots. Trees that were cut were left with an ample stump which had enough time before inundation to sprout new sapling growth and create natural fish cover.

Ken Sims, a fishery biologist for the Corps of Engineers' Mobile District, shouldered much of the burden for the fish attracting features of the Tenn/Tom. Sims says, "We tried to leave timber standing in six feet of water or less so that it wouldn't present as great a navigation hazard when the trees rotted and broke off at the water line. Our fish attractors are essentially stump-fields in water ten feet or more near deeper water. Stumps were left with a maximum height of four feet covered by at least six feet of water. There was also substantial regrowth on the stump before they were inundated."

The Tenn/Tom Waterway represents the ideal fish/cover ratio but it won't last indefinitely. Natural cover wears away very quickly and the loss has to be re-introduced by the placement of artificial cover. Most states have an active fish attractor program that is paying handsome dividends because fish attractors attract fish!

The most comprehensive fish study in history was conducted on Kentucky's Lake Barkley on the use and types of fish attractors. Various conclusions were reached but the overriding theme was that 45 times more fish were found around attractors than in open water! After the study, these sites were marked with buoys and I caught many a crappie by going from one buoy to another and never cranking up the motor.

A Tennessee Valley Authority fishery crew plants a brush attractor on Lake Barkley and marks the spot with a white buoy. Don't hesitate to fish a marked-off fish attractor......they'll produce crappie in spite of heavy pressure.

Working fish attractors is a good pattern on any lake, especially if you're new to the lake. Sure, I know that everybody else is going to fish a marked-off fish attractor, but hey, they'll produce fish day in and day out. So don't pass them by because they're being fished hard.

Which brings up the question of marking the attractor. Of course, government agencies are honor-bound to mark their attractor sites for the sake of the general public. That's the way it should be. Most weekend or vacationing anglers don't have the time or the inclination to spend winter weekends sinking brush into a lake. They probably wouldn't know where to place it anyway and it also happens to be illegal without the proper permit from the authorities. Therefore, this group of fishermen depends on the state's efforts to improve their fishing. And they also fish around other floating objects in the hopes that it is marking a crappie hideout. Sometimes it is and sometimes it's tied to a commercial fisherman's trotline or gill net. But nothing makes my crappie-fishing friends madder than to find a boat anchored over one of their favorite (it's always the favorite) brushpile that they've worked long and hard to get into position.

You can appreciate that attitude if you've wrestled with a load of brush or tires on a cold day or driven stakes in 40 degree water with waders on! Brrr! Yes, it's hard work but imminently satisfying when it starts producing fillets. But should you mark the site? If it's going to disrupt your day to find a stranger (No, friends can't fish it either—in fact they're worse) on the baited hole, don't mark it. At least don't mark it in an obvious manner. The old triangulation method of three objects on the shoreline converging on a common spot is still excellent. Two objects in a line are also good and just one may suffice. A treetop laying in the water is a favorite of mine and I use it to point to a planted brushpile about 30 to 60 feet from its end. The set-up will produce fish for several consecutive weeks in the spring and in the fall. Migrating crappie will stop first in the deeper water brushpile before moving into the branches of the treetop in shallower depths. In bays and coves where this situation exists, crappie will remain until warmer temperatures in the summer or colder climes in the fall move them. The same set on a river channel can be productive year round.

The advantage of the pointing tree is that it is close to the spot. The closer you can mark, the better. Any latitude one way or another could result in precious minutes lost trying to make contact and if the water is clear and less than 10 feet deep, you may disturb the fish by running over them.

An accurate mark that is easy to read is the solution. Easier said than done sometimes. I've lost track of attractors because of inadequate locating devices many times......so many times that I think overall it may be best to tie a bottle or styrofoam block on it and let others fish it if they choose! I feel the same way about stumps. A cane or willow stick in the top of a stump is invaluable when the water rises in the spring. Let everybody fish it! At least, I'm going to catch my share there too! I've seen too many fishermen who thought they knew exactly where a stump was and miss it by 10 yards on their initial casts. Unless you're fishing the same stump everyday, it's going to appear to be in a different spot because of changing water levels.

Even fishing guides forget where they've put an attractor and they can't afford to be blundering around looking for a lost brushpile. It just doesn't sound good to a client if the guide says "There's a brushpile here somewhere." For his one hundred or more dollars a day, the client expects exact location and positive results! So guides will often mark with a floating object such as a natural stick or wood chip that doesn't attract attention. Because of this, guides simply do not like to take local residents out even though they've contracted his services. He much prefers an out-of-state tourist who only visits once or twice a year. The guide knows that the locals will mentally fix the location and move in later to check it out. Which means that he has to continually add new sites to his territory. Brush attractors are usually only good for three years so constant replacement is necessary anyway. Plus, they tend to move with high water and from relocation by other fishermen.

However, the best marked fish-attractor site in the lake isn't going to be worth a Mexican peso if it's in the wrong area. I've seen beautiful sets of brush placed on mud flats that I'll guarantee will never harbor a crappie. They're just not going to use sites that don't meet their requirements, even where cover is sparse. Conversely, I've put in attractors that have never harbored a crappie at "perfect" places. Trial and error is the only solution. Not all of them work for

Tie the anchor snug to the base of the brush.

reasons known only to those with scaly sides, but most of them will if you'll study maps and use a depth sounder to make precise placements.

On deep, clear steep-sided highland lakes which have severe drawdowns to winter levels (30 to 60 feet from summer to winter pool), fish attractors can also be productive and the process is greatly simplified because there's only one or two types of sites that will work. Because of drawdown, all of the attractors should be placed on dry ground during the winter months. There are exceptions to this rule but it's been my experience that crappie are rarely going to be found over 35 feet deep.

The sites to look for are at the heads of creeks and coves. Place the brush at elevations which will put 5, 10, and 15 feet of water over them as the pool starts to rise in March and April. Keep in mind that shallow water brushpiles will have to be fished by casting from a good distance away because of the clear water. With several brushpiles stair-stepped at different depths, fish should hold for two or three months in this area if they traditionally use it in the spring. Not all coves or tributaries appeal to crappie. Concentrate your efforts on those that are known to yield stringers of papermouths. Productive spring cover will also produce again in the fall.

Other sites for brushpiles, tires, treetops, and stake beds in highland lakes are ledges on the channel bluffs. All bluffs have one or more ledges that fish will hold on if there's some sort of cover. One small bush is often all that's necessary to entertain large numbers of crappie. Salt these ledges in the winter when the lake is low and you'll have an excellent summer and winter concentration point. Concentrate your efforts on bluffs along the main channel of the lake rather than in the tributaries.

Other potential areas for fish-attracting cover require more study of maps and on-the-water research with a depth finder. High spots, old roadbeds, islands, house foundations, and cemeteries are all prime spots. And any highland lake, no matter how steep throughout its length, will have some shallow gravel and clay points that can be laced with fish attractors and be productive in early spring and fall.

LOWLAND LAKES

Fishermen on lowland lakes profit year round by the addition of fish attractors. Their network of channels, ditches, roadbeds, highspots, flats and modest sloping banks make them eligible for an attractor just about anywhere. Only trouble is, you shouldn't put them just anywhere. Try to locate a change in depth. For spring and fall, the change may only be a difference of a foot or two in the backs of bays. An exception to the depth-change rule is gravel banks in shallow water. I've had excellent success on practically all of my brush sets when placed on a bank with small gravel on it. Not all lowland lakes will have gravel but if yours does, you can bet crappie will spawn on it in the spring. Sweeten it with a brushpile and you are in business......but have several that you can visit so that you can move when the action slows or a boat approaches.

There's an old axiom that applies to fish hides—"if it's working, don't fix it." If a stump row or dropoff is producing crappie, "Don't fix it!" Don't add more brush to make it better. You may produce the opposite and ruin what had once been a fish producer. So leave a good thing alone and don't add additional brush.

Another worthwhile ploy for shallow water activity is stake beds. Of course you can preconstruct stake beds and use them in deeper water but let's talk about driving individual stakes into the lake bottom. Bill McLemore, Kentucky's fish biologist, prefers to tightly group his stakes which almost touch each other. I've caught enough crappie out of them on Lake Barkley to know that they work and work well. Al Hamilton, who owns and operates a marina and resort on Tennessee's famed Reelfoot Lake, takes a different, but no less effective, tact. He drives single stakes three or four feet apart in rows which allows anglers to catch a fish or two around each stake.

A single stake or stick-up may hold several crappie and will yield a fish or two on return visits.

Stake beds placed along the edge of a creek channel and extending into the creek bed will hold fish in the spring on their way to spawning grounds and on their way back to deep water; then again in the fall.

Stake beds are best in water less than six feet deep, although they can be effective in deeper water by preconstructing the bed on land and anchoring each corner with a concrete block. Preconstruction also has an advantage in shallow water where rock and gravel bottoms predominate and stakes can't be driven. Driven stakes have the advantage in that the size of the bed can be adjusted and additional stakes can be added each winter to a productive bed.

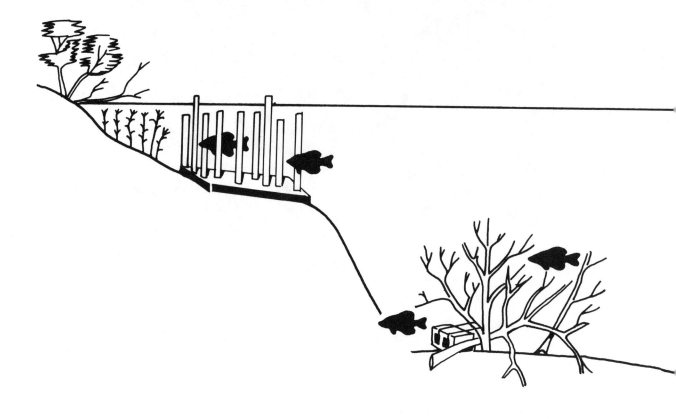

A brushpile in water six to ten feet deep along a migration route produces fish consistently for several weeks in the spring and again in the fall. Tie concrete blocks snug against the branches if using wire so that water movement doesn't wear it out prematurely.

Traditionally, cedar trees have been used for crappie mats and they still work but hardwoods such as oak, hickory, maple, locust, hackberry and osage orange are better. Birch and willow are also excellent as are fruit trees such as apple, peach, plum and pear. Availability usually determines the choice but remember not to cut the vegetation along the shoreline......bring it from home!

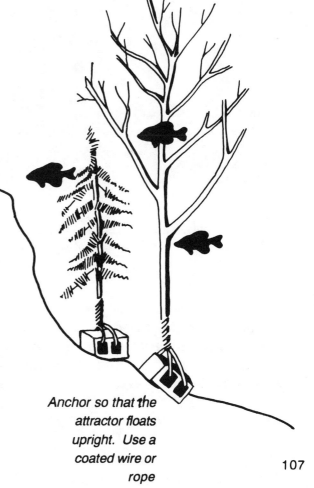

Fish Attractors placed on a creek channel dropoff with the proper water depths are the ultimate locale for consistent angling. The proper depth will vary with individual lakes and seasons and you may have to experiment until a productive zone is determined. A good parameter for most of the U.S. is from 8 to 38 feet. Look for a dropoff or breakline within this range which has a 4- to 10-foot rather sharp change (within one boat length). If the channel is deep enough and has sufficient current, crappie may remain all year. However, it's best to have deep water attractors for summer and winter angling and middle depth attractors for spring and fall.

Anchor so that the attractor floats upright. Use a coated wire or rope

107

My experience has been with groups of stakes set wider apart than those favored by McLemore. They'll all work. In fact, Bill Pearson, owner of Cedar Creek Dock on Tennessee's Old Hickory Lake, maintains that a single isolated stake will hold some fish.

Driving stakes is hard work and because it's usually done in the winter, it's also cold. Especially if you drop your hammer. Stakes aren't hard to find if there's any kind of wood-working mill nearby. Two dollars will probably buy all that you'll want to put out in one winter. And here is a case that refutes an earlier statement that I made about not adding any more brush if it's already

This is cold but rewarding work on a winter day as long as you don't drop the hammer! Hardwood stakes obtained from a local sawmill are randomly driven to different heights. The lake is at winter pool and will be five feet higher come spring. Don't forget where all the work took place! Use markers on the shoreline and plot the information on a map.

working. If a stake bed produces fish, enlarge or lengthen it the following year. Stake beds will only last about three years anyway, so it's a good idea to annually replenish the site. Or you may opt to drive another group 50 feet away in slightly deeper water. If the bed doesn't produce, either forget about it or come back and try it for bass. Oftentimes lunker largemouths fall in love with these beds that for some reason don't appeal to crappie.

During dry springs, crappie may spawn before rising water levels get into shallow water or shoreline cover. For this reason, it's imperative that you have attractors in mid-depths of 8 to 12 feet. Ideally, you should have all three depth ranges covered—shallow (less than 5 feet), midway (6 to 12 feet) and deep (13 to 25 feet). Rarely, will they ever be deeper than 25 feet.

If crappie spawn before the lake level gets to the shallow cover, which most anglers depend on for springtime action, the fisherman who has gone to the trouble of putting out brushpiles will catch most of the fish. And it may last for 6 to 10 weeks covering the prespawn, spawn and postspawn activities. On the other hand, if the lake rises and floods into surrounding woods and thickets, the crappie will follow the high water and attempt to spawn in the flooded territory. Fish attractors during a spring flood will work once again as crappie retreat to deeper water when the water level starts to fall.

After the spring rush is over and the spawning ritual is completed, schools of crappie begin to return to the creek channel dropoffs they favor until late summer. Fish attractors are harder to locate properly on the dropoffs because they may slide into the channel and be too deep or they may be too far from the edge of the dropoff. But don't let that discourage your attempt. This is too good a place to pass up. Do a lot of homework with maps and a depthfinder to locate a zone that drops sharply from 4 to 10 feet and has some sort of irregular feature such as another channel intersection, stumps or an outside bend. Attractors should be placed at different intervals along the creek until they reach the main river channel because fish migrate to the river channel by July and then return in the fall for the winter.

Thus, on lowland lakes it is possible to keep crappie relating to attractors all year long if they're in the right location. That's not so on highland lakes but it can be true of midland lakes, at least in their upper reaches where they exhibit characteristics of lowland impoundments. It's also not true of old river and oxbow lakes where crappie tend to "suspend" in open water. In fact, this is an environment where there is a wealth of natural cover and virtually no need to install attractors.

The importance of placing some kind of crappie-attracting device can't be stressed enough where cover is lacking. Obviously, a number of lakes don't need any additional encouragement. They'll either have acres and acres of inundated timber or aquatic plants. When I moved to Decatur, Alabama on Wheeler Reservoir of the great TVA chain of lakes, the first thing I hoped to do was get some brushpiles in before spring. Mike Jones, an old fishing buddy living in nearby Huntsville, offered this advice when I told him of my intentions: "You'll be wasting your time fooling with that. The crappie on Wheeler stay in the milfoil beds which are all over the lake."

Massive Guntersville Lake, immediately upstream of Wheeler, also has acres and acres of grass in its shallow bays. Guide Billy Ledbetter says, "I've put out several big brushpiles the past two years and I haven't caught any crappie out of them yet! The grass is the reason—they just won't use the brush—at least not in water less than 10 feet deep. They might use it if it were placed on deep dropoffs."

So, if you've analyzed your favorite body of water and decided it needs attractors or that you need to put some in to help increase your catch, the next question is: What do I make them out of and what configuration should they be? The answer lies in your own creativity because there are countless variations and depends primarily on the availability of materials. Christmas trees are the old standby for many fishermen who collect them after the holidays and take a boatload to the lake. They're readily available and it's the right time of year to put them out. Probably more crappie have been caught around cedar trees than any other artificially placed cover so who am I to disagree, but I prefer to use hardwood such as oak, maple, hickory, poplar, locust, osage orange etc. Actually, whatever I can find under a powerline clearing or in the wake of a logging operation is what I'll use.

Locust is a personal favorite and I also like willow. Bob Holmes prefers birch while Jim Abers, a guide on Buggs Island Lake, uses sweet gum. Keep in mind that the lake's governing authorities frown on removing shoreline brush and trees and some agencies such as the Corps of Engineers require a permit to place fish attractors in their lakes.

Tires function extremely well as fish attractors; they are durable, easily obtainable and will last longer than the binding it takes to lash a group together. They are also a good medium for fishing clubs to work with because they're cheap, available in quantities, and they require a good bit of manual labor. Even steel belted tires won't sink properly without two or three large (3-inch diameter) holes drilled in the tread. This is a difficult job. And they still require a measure of concrete in each.

Small pyramids of eight to ten tires are the favored size which are assembled on land and transported by boat. A small working barge used by state Game and Fish agencies for waterfowl management work is ideal if it can be borrowed. To make a larger attractor, the pyramids can be tied together in a continuing train. To date, the best binding for tires has been a polyethylene plastic band which is available at most hardware stores.

To make a tire attractor even better, add brush......it's a little more icing on the cake. And don't be afraid to experiment with different configurations of tires and the choice of locations in the lake. The same can be said for brush......let your imagination be your guide and try to build a better fish attractor. Crappie will beat a path to your door!

Scott Wicker of Eddyville, Kentucky, plies his trade on Lake Barkley in western Kentucky. Scott conceived the idea of using discarded five-gallon buckets, filling them with sand and rocks, sticking cane or willows into the rocks and dropping them overboard.

George Warren, who fishes out of Leisure Cruise Marina on Lake Barkley, uses wooden pallets tied together with stakes and adds brush. Some of his affairs get pretty elaborate. Norm Brantley, creel census clerk for Kentucky's Fish and Wildlife Resources, has made an in-depth study of fish attractors. One of his ideas is unique in design and triggered by the availability of a certain type of anchor. The anchor is a round metal plate with teeth like an old gear to which he has individually wired long 6-foot wooden stakes. When he places this in the water, the stakes float above their anchor and will "give" when hit by a plug or jig which reduces hang-ups.

Like I've said before, only your imagination, and perhaps laziness, is standing in the way of catching more crappie with fish attractors.

Spring!

Chapter X

About the middle of February, even in the northern states, fishermen begin to take notice of longer days and warmer temperatures. In the South, February is prime time for anglers seeking crappie, which are still on deep water structures but are becoming more active and restless. Usually a week long respite from winter weather stirs both fish and fisherman out of hibernation. Be ready to fish during this warm spell because some great catches can be made until the inevitable cold front shuts things down completely.

Cold fronts are the nemesis of crappie fishermen in spring. Just as soon as activity picks up and fish begin to move towards shallow water, a front sends them back to their winter holding areas. These in and out movements are frustrating but they are the nature of things. Some comfort can be taken in knowing that the next front will be less severe and spring is struggling to make her annual appearance.

There are actually two springs for the crappie fisherman to consider—early spring which can begin in February and extend through March and late spring which comes in the last of March and extends into May and June.

EARLY SPRING

As water temperatures climb out of the 30-degree bracket into the 40-degree range, crappie begin to react to the slightest differential. Both vertical and horizontal movements occur. In deep, clear lakes where cover is minimal, crappie may only make a vertical ascent to sun-warmed waters along a sheer bluff or bridgespan. Any kind of tree that's fallen into the water on a bluff is a veritable magnet at this time of year. An angler's approach has to be cautious. Water clarity won't permit getting within the range of a hand-held pole. Casting with ultra-light gear and $1/16$- or $1/32$-ounce jigs is preferred although a minnow fished under a sliding cork and drifted into the treetop can be deadly.

Two-pound-test line is necessary to cast the diminutive jigs and maintain minimum line visibility. Clear water crappie are spooky and the presentation has to be perfect. Experiment via the countdown method until the depth of the school is determined.

Not all of the fallen treetops hold crappie; some will be holding largemouth and smallmouth bass and these bullies will drive crappie out of a treetop! A cold front may not drive them out of a treetop but it will push them deeper. Two to three days after the front, they'll move back into the shallower branches and if warm weather continues, the migration into the tributaries or on to shallow flats begins. Spring has Sprung!

Spawning sites on canyon, plateau and highland lakes and, to a lesser degree, midland and flood control reservoirs, are at a premium. Which is why fish attractors pay such tremendous dividends in the spring. It's important to have brushpiles staggered from below winter pool to summer pool. Sure, it amounts to a lot of work because of the extreme drawdown of many impoundments but it'll be worth it, because crappie are going to spawn when the water temperature gets right regardless of the pool level. During a mild winter, spawning may take place before the body of water rises to summer pool levels.

On mammoth Kentucky Lake, where thousands of anglers flock in April and May for their annual "filling the freezer" trip, the celebrated move into shoreline cover hasn't materialized the last few years. Crappie are spawning in March and early April before the water level reaches the traditional spawning grounds.

Bob Holmes says that spawning in Kentucky Lake has gotten earlier and earlier since 1965. Warm days and more importantly, warm nights, can quickly send water temperatures into the range which triggers the spawn. Scientists postulate that this universal warming trend will continue.

This change in spawning behavior is an ill omen for most crappie fishermen who simply do not know how to catch fish in open water and who do not have the time to make a mid-winter trip to put out fish attractors. That's why the good Lord made crappie guides! For a relatively few dollars, he can teach you to catch fish in open water on brushpiles and cedar trees he's put in during the past few winters. Two fishermen splitting the cost of a top guide is an excellent investment. (See chapter on Guides.)

Bob Holmes says, "I just can't say enough about putting in some type of cover. A good rule of thumb is about one of every three sets will pay off consistently. My favorite wood for brushpiles is birch—it's light and easy to carry. It mosses up quickly which is important, and it will last two years in shallow water and three to four years in deeper water. Willow is also good but there's a rule of thirds about willow—you'll lose 1/3 when it's cut, another 1/3 as you drag it to the lake and you'll finally get 1/3 of it in the lake!"

Early spring crappie movements begin with the first migration out of their winter sanctuaries. Invariably this move is initially vertical in lowland, midland, canyon, and flood control lakes just as it is in highland impoundments. "Suspended" fish simply ascend to the top layer of water being warmed by the sun. Holmes calls this the "awakening" when crappie move up to the top of ledges and "sun" in six to eight feet of water. If a school is on a deep dropoff covered with stumps, they disperse to the edge of the dropoff and swim slowly around the stumps and also back onto the flats. They'll stay in this situation for several days if the weather remains stable. When it changes, the school will reform on the dropoff or ledge or they may "suspend" away from the dropoff but at the same depth in relation to the stumps.

"Crappie will hit when they return to a deep water-holding area in response to a cold front," says Holmes. "With a 'do nothing' approach, I'll hover right over the school and fish a tube jig with Fish Formula just as slowly as possible. In fact, I'll try to hold the jig motionless until one sucks it in. Now, if the front is severe, the school will tighten into a ball and descend even deeper. When my 4-ID shows a dense wad of fish below their normal holding zone, I know they are inactive and very hard to catch. In other words, it's time to go to the house!"

Ronnie Guyton reports an almost identical scenario on the chain of Tennessee/Tombigbee Waterway lakes which are lowland reservoirs with a strong river channel influence. On sunny days in early spring, schools of crappie come to the top of the ledges along the river channel and in the major tributaries. They'll change depths throughout the day.

Ronnie prefers a ten-foot fiberglass pole, a simple line holder and a handful of Slater's jigs which feature a deer-hair body with a sliver of reflective tinsel. Color of the jig is not as important as size; the $\frac{1}{8}$ and $\frac{1}{4}$ ounce sizes seem to take bigger crappie for Ronnie but most anglers use $\frac{1}{16}$ or $\frac{1}{32}$ ounce sizes or small minnows.

This is a great time to catch a limit of big slabs if you're in tune with their movements, which takes regular fishing. By regular I mean three or four times a week! At least two times anyway! I realize that most people can't go that often unless it's the weekend and then the spring crowds are churning the water. You have to have advance information from buddies that have fished a few days before, a marina operator who caters to fishermen or a local baitshop. Don't be too specific about exact location (which treetop, cove, bank)—simply ask "how deep?" The most close-mouthed fisherman will often share that bit of information without feeling threatened. If you can get more, fine, but let them volunteer what they will and when your turn comes to help a fellow fisherman, do so.

Isn't it disgusting to have a wise guy showing off a stringer of giant white perch respond to a legitimate inquiry about how he achieved his success with "Well, I caught most of 'em in the top lip," or "On the left side of the boat!" Those replies are at least creative. The real yoyos say, "In the lake" or "On the hook!" while guffawing loudly to their partner.

Armed beforehand with the knowledge of "how deep," a crappie angler can lay out Saturday's game plan and expect to come away with a mess of fish that'll draw a crowd around the marina. Then he'll have to fend off questions such as "Exactly what treetop did you say they were in?"

After the move vertically to the ledges and all things are proceeding normally (no cold fronts) the next migration will be to the mouths of creeks for those crappie in the main channel. For those already in the major creeks because of their depth and current, the first move is to the mouths of coves, sloughs, small creeks, and pockets just off a creek channel. Not all of them will move, some will stay on a ledge or dropoff with good cover. The second movement finds crappie all over the lake and they'll remain in staggered order

SPRING MIGRATION PATTERN

This is a typical creek on a lowland reservoir. Although the map leaves out many of the bottom features, it does outline the most important. . . .the migration route or old creek channel. Crappie will use this as a highway to their spawning grounds in the head of the main creek and also the secondary creeks.

Start the search in the bends of the channel and stay away from the straight stretches. Pay particular attention to what appears to be three "high spots" (1,2,3) in the creek channel. . . .these are potential crappie goldmines!

For those without electronic gear, start fishing on the banks where the creek channel comes in close (A,B). At area B, be sure and fish the adjacent cove—it looks like ideal spawning territory. Area C also looks promising—a high spot in the creek bed just before going under a railroad bridge which is normally flanked by riprapped embankments, a favorite habitat for early spring crappie.

While working the railroad bridge, note that there's a creek entering on each side (D,E) although the channel of the creek isn't showing on the map. Here you can do two things: 1. Go as far up these creeks as possible and fish available cover for spawning fish; 2. Wait until the afternoon and devote a couple of hours to the depth finder and those unmapped creek channels to determine their course. Where they intersect with the main creek channel is Crappie City!

Proceeding upstream under the railroad bridge, the first thing that jumps out is a small island, (F), which the channel hits on both ends and two or three larger islands, (G), just a little further. Islands this close to deeper water are prime and deserve a large amount of attention.

The highway bridge, (H), also deserves attention because it will hold fish along the sides of the road embankment where there is brush or willow in the water.

Beyond Point H we lose the outline of the creek channel but it may be evident visually from treelines, brush or weedlines. Fish as close to it (the creek) as possible for as far as it goes.

Keep in mind that the spring migration is conditional upon cold fronts and heavy rains which move crappie back and forth during the spawning ritual. You don't have to start at Point A if you have reason to believe that fish are in the shoreline bushes; go there first and then work out if they're not.

The IMPORTANT thing to do is to develop a GAME PLAN before you get to the lake.

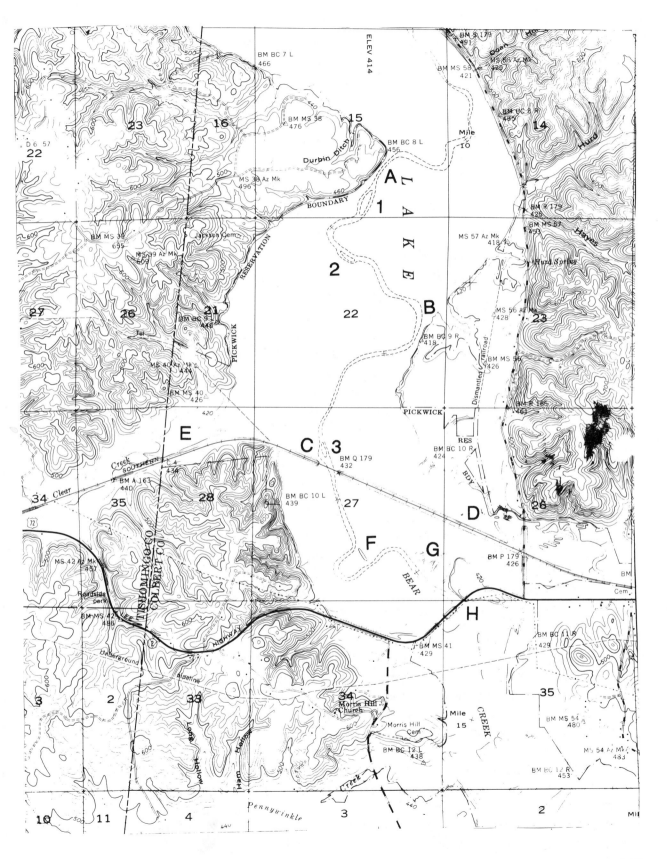

117

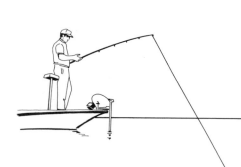

Position 1 - Crappie in this position (shallow water less than 6') are aggressive and easily caught by minnows, flies, road runners, or jigs. They'll remain in the shallows until a cold front moves them out or the spawning ritual is completed.

Position 2 - Crappie on the edge of a dropoff (8'-18') are poised to make their move into the shallows. They are waiting for optimum conditions of water temperature and clarity. This position serves a multiple springtime role as a staging area for spawning fish, a retreat during mild cold fronts, and the first stopover for females after spawning.

Position 3 - Crappie in this stance are usually tightly grouped, deep (below 20'), and suffering from a severe cold front. If the front persists, they may move back to the main body of the lake. A few can be caught by holding a minnow or tube jig loaded with Fish Formula in the school until one reluctantly sucks it in. When you can catch a mess for supper when they're in this position, you're on your way to becoming a real crappie fisherman!

until after spawning which protects against a calamitous loss of the entire hatch. It also stretches out the shallow water season and makes for more satisfied fishermen, guides, minnow dealers, and Chambers of Commerce!

Some lakes, apparently unable to cope with the amount and types of commercial nets in their waters, have lost this valuable springtime boost to their local economies.

If the first spring movement is an "awakening," the second movement would have to be a "staging." Crappie rally to staging areas where they'll hold until conditions (water, temperature, clarity) are optimum before dispersing into the shallows to drop their eggs. Males are already in the shallows making preparations for the females who remain in the staging area.

Holmes refers to this movement as a pre-spawn pattern and he looks for the fish to come into his "staging" brushpiles which have 8 to 10 feet of water over them. They may, however, elect to spawn in these brushpiles if the lake doesn't rise into traditional spawning territory. After spawning, they'll return to these same brushpiles and remain there as long as water temperatures remain cool. This is when the hard work of winter pays off. The guys catching all the fish after the spawn are those with fish attractors in 8 to 10 feet of water. Casting with jigs, tightlining with minnows or using a cork with a minnow all produce equally well in this situation.

OPEN WATER METHODS

Drifting, dragging and trolling are effective open water methods during the movement to the second staging area. Large expanses of water can be covered with these methods which involve the simultaneous fishing of several poles arranged spider-leg fashion around the boat. As many as 12 poles can be effectively fished after a certain amount of experience, although the coordination required to keep that many poles in the water is taxing. Start with two or three per person and work up.

Names vary for these styles of fishing depending on geographic location but they either use the wind, an electric trolling motor or an outboard for power. The longest poles may stretch 20 feet which cuts a wide swath across potential holding spots. When a fish is caught, throw out a marker and circle back through. If the fish are "stacked" along a breakline or cover edge, several fish can be taken on each pass. For some reason, only the pass in one certain direction will produce consistently. You simply won't catch as many, if any, on the return pass via the same route as you caught coming down.

Equipment for these open water methods consists of poles up to 20 feet as I've mentioned, but the ones on the sides should be of different lengths to help prevent tangling lines in a turn. Reels aren't necessary but a set of good pole holders are vital. Fairly heavy monofilament line is employed and tube jigs have replaced live minnows because they're less trouble.

Most multi-pole boats or "spider rigs," as they are commonly referred to, have an array of pole holders to suit the fisherman's personal needs. Jim Fowler of Tunica, Mississippi, uses a numbering system on his pontoon boat so that he can quickly tell his partners what call to answer first. Of course, spinning, spincasting and casting rods and reels can also be used and at least one or more are handy as short poles.

While minnows will catch fish equally as well as jigs, the expense and bother of rebaiting has shifted most addicts to artificial lures. Consider the price of minnows and the loss of 300 to 500 during a day's fishing and you're looking at a bait of money! With ten poles in the water and three hooks on each line, it takes time to bait and rebait. If only three lines are out, then it's not such a big deal. Select a light wire hook so that it will straighten out of a stump easily and

A spider rig covers a wide expanse of water at different depths with an array of jigs and minnows. It is a method endorsed by crappie tournament fishermen who are on a lake for the first time and a number of crappie have to be caught in order to do well in the tournament. For that reason, it's also good for the average fisherman visiting a new lake. However, the method is not easy to employ without a lot of practice.

will impale the minnow through the lips. Fish as near the bottom as practical and start in deeper water early in the morning and work shallower as the day progresses. Line test is not critical although most prefer over 10-pound test. Jig colors, whether tube, tail hair or twister tail, vary according to factors such as water clarity and the time of day. Multi-pole fishing permits experimenting with a number of colors to determine the most effective for that day. Today the terrific color might be hot pink and tomorrow sky blue! That's what makes it fun! Remember when color selection meant black, white or yellow?

George and Gena Darnell of Kuttawa, Kentucky have been experimenting with a Color-C-Lector on Lake Barkley. Results indicate that it provides a definite advantage to the fisherman. But you'd better have a wide assortment of colors; the C-Lector may suggest blue/green in the morning, purple at noon and burnt orange at sunset!

Prime Time! The big females are in the shallows!

INTO THE SHALLOWS

The final movement into the shallows is the one most coveted by crappie fishermen. . . .they're in shoreline cover! Now's the time to load the boat! Without a doubt, it is the time that crappie are most vulnerable, whether it be in the reeds of Minnesota, mesquite bushes in Arizona, cypress trees in Louisiana or standing timber in Mississippi.

Spawning by individual females only takes a few days if no cold fronts interrupt the process. The spawning season is much longer than that because not all of the females come in at the same time. There can also be as much as a four- to six-week range from year to year in which the spawning activity peaks.

In other words, it can be awfully hard to plan an annual vacation in advance to coincide with the mating behavior of a fish! A helpful hint—when scheduling with your boss, try not to put down an actual date. Condition your vacation leave as dependent on: "When dogwoods are in bloom,"; or "When tom turkeys are gobbling,"; or "When morel mushrooms are up,"; or, as a last resort, "When groundhogs are breeding!" Use anything tied to the vagaries of spring weather that will allow you to get to the lake at the proper time. You can look for another job when you return!

Spawning crappie are the easiest to catch but they aren't a sure thing! Number one, they're not everywhere. Only certain stretches of shoreline cover will be productive. If you've paid attention to the migration routes during the previous weeks, it's simple, they'll be spread out on either side of where the migration route hits the spawning cover. Migration routes are usually determined by a change in elevation of the bottom of lowland, midland and flood control reservoirs. Creek channels are the most likely highways but others in wide use are ditches, stump rows, weedlines, fences, and standing timber. Rarely will crappie cross expansive flats without some irregularity present to guide them. They like to move along some sort of structure.

If this is your first trip to a lake and you thought migration routes were for waterfowl, try to get an underwater contour map from a marina or baitshop. Study the map and circle the shallow areas where a creek channel comes closest to the shoreline. This is an excellent place to start prospecting. Fish at a rapid pace but fish thoroughly. Don't waste a lot of time in an area that happens to yield a straggler. Continue down the bank until you find a concentration but don't go more than 100 yards without action before turning back to the starting point and fishing the other way. Be forever alert along the way for the telltale tip of a brushpile lying in open water just off the shoreline. They prefer these to the thicker cover and the brushpile may be hosting a crappie convention!

OTHER LAKES

Highland, plateau, and canyon lakes exhibit migration routes such as road-beds, rock fences, ridges or long rocky points. With the exception of underwater ridges, these can be determined visually by boating along the shoreline although a good map will save a lot of gas. Check these migration routes with ultralight jigs and start way out and work into the shoreline. They may be hugging the structure or suspended above it. Trolling at right angles to the migration route is also a good method.

However, the easiest thing to do in spring on the deep clear lakes, whether they are in Arizona or Tennessee, is to motor to the head of a tributary......all the way to the end. Look for any kind of cover (natural or artificial) on a shallow bank and start fishing. Cover is usually at such a premium in this type of lake that any woody structure will cause fish to concentrate there. It also helps to find a tributary with some "color" to it from spring rains. With "color," you don't have to be as careful in your approach to the cover. If the crappie aren't yet in the shallow cover, they are suspended in open water in the tributary. A diligent search with the depth finder or by trolling will help locate an errant school.

Not all lakes have well defined migration routes. Natural lakes such as Reelfoot and Okeechobee are saucer shaped, shallow and open. Sometimes a ditch or slight change in bottom contour can be found but fishing patterns are usually determined by the amount and type of vegetation.

Early spring fishing normally means trolling or drifting through the deepest water of the lake for suspended schools. As the water warms, the schools disperse toward spawning territory. Even in natural lakes there are staging areas.

At Reelfoot Lake in northwest Tennessee, drift fishing begins over submerged trees in 12 feet of water. The next staging area is to trees with four to six feet of water around them and then finally to trees in less than two feet of water. In many sections of Reelfoot, crappie can't get to woody cover because of dense aquatic growth. Here they will actually spawn on the root systems of lily pads and mulefoot bonnets.

Bob Holmes tells how he fishes the Earthquake Lake in late spring. "With a long pole and jig I'll simply start in the trees or the mulefoot bonnets and go and go and go! When I catch one, I slow down and fish the area more thoroughly. If it produces additional fish, I'll mark the spot with a cane so that I can come back later. Generally, a hot spot will contain a consistent size of fish—they may average six ounces or twelve ounces but practically all of them will look like they had the same parents.

"There are some things to look for in the seemingly endless acres of bonnets. Note anything different, no matter how slight......a clump of bonnets that's a little taller than the others or standing off by itself; a stump or log just under the surface; or merely an opening or slight indentation. Old duck blinds are one of the best spawning sites on Reelfoot."

EQUIPMENT

Equipment is a simple affair when the crappie are in shallow water cover......a 10- to 14-foot pole and a minnow or a tube jig are all that's required. A tube jig is more effective than other types because it has action even when holding it still in the cover, a technique often successful after a cold front. Extremely thick cover may necessitate the addition of a sliding cork and a lead sinker above the hook to help guide a minnow through the maze of branches.

Wading fishermen score heavily at this time of year if the lake bottom is firm and even. A wader can negotiate the toughest of tangles that would stop a boat, although I've seen fishermen plow their boat straight into a wall of brush and start fishing!

Fortunately, the spring spawning season is not an orderly process or the population would be reduced to dangerously low levels. Cold fronts play their part, the major part, but other factors come into play that can be even more disruptive—high water and/or muddy water.

HIGH WATER

Rising water which floods into "new ground" can be a mixed blessing. Crappie love to forage on what has suddenly become a new smorgasbord in town. All kinds of worms, insects, crayfish and other delectables are now on the menu! Armies of fish scatter over the fertile feeding grounds to take advantage of the largess.

In the spring, follow rising water levels into newly inundated territory.

Fishermen should do the same. Go into the woods and fields as far as water depth permits. You may want to park the boat and wade. A pole, fish stringer and a pocket full of jigs are all that's needed. Black seems to be the best jig color because of its resemblance to insects but other colors will work because of the voracious feeding by the fish. Watch out for snakes that are attracted to the flopping of fish on a string!

Holmes says, "Go out in the fields with 'em! I use a stiff fly rod and tightline jigs around stumps, brush, trees, ditches, and fence rows. I like a jig with a slow beat to the tail like Charlie Brewer's slider grubs. Catching fish means getting right in the middle of flooded trees and bushes. I do this by pulling the jig up to the rod tip and letting it drop straight down into an opening the size of a coffee cup. Because of the heavy cover and the need to get a big crappie out of the tangle quickly, a stiff pole is absolutely necessary.

"In the winter when I'm putting out fish attractors and I see a stump on dry land that I know will have crappie around it during high water, I stick a cane in it so I can find it when the time comes."

"When the time comes" is a key phrase. According to research studies by TVA fishery biologist Dr. Tom Forsythe, crappie are not right behind the advance of flood waters. They wait two or three days suspended at the edge of the vegetation before "going in." It seems that they want to be sure of the water levels before leaving their deep water sanctuary. Once they do make the move, they'll remain in the floodplain as long as the water level remains stable or spawning is completed. When it starts to fall, crappie don't hesitate, they move immediately back towards deeper water. Along the way they'll stop at ambush points created by an obstruction such as duckblinds, beaverdams, fences, buildings, and logs. Not all of them make it back to their original watercourse, many are stranded in bottomland lakes and sloughs—Mother Nature's restocking plan!

An unfortunate spring flood that lasts for weeks could result in the loss of the entire spawn. Egg masses are left high and dry when flood waters recede. Oxbows and old river chutes along the Mississippi, Missouri, Arkansas, Ohio, and the Mobile Delta are particularly prone to this event but it's been going on for eons.

Although lowland lakes, flood-control reservoirs, and river-influenced lakes suffer more from the effects of spring floods, both highland and midland types will be affected, but not as adversely.

Carneal Walden of Nashville, Tennessee, is quick to take advantage of high water levels on his backyard Percy Priest Lake, a midland impoundment of the Stones River. Carneal can catch fish from a boat with the best but he prefers to fish on foot in the spring. If the water's normal, he wades in the backs of bays on shallow flats salted with brushpiles.

When the lake floods, Carneal says, "After the water gets into the trees, I'll put on my chest waders and fish parallel with the edge of a treeline. I fish on the same shallow banks with broken rocks, sand, gravel, and stumps that are productive when its normal. Use a light spinning or spincast outfit with six-pound test and a cork with a minnow or jig. My favorite is a white or chartreuse twister-tail jig in $1/16$- or $1/32$-ounce sizes."

MUDDY WATER

Nothing is more demoralizing to a crappie fisherman than muddy water. Especially if he's just driven 100 miles to his favorite lake! I've pulled up to a lake or river, noted its coffee-with-cream color and turned right around for home.

I still don't like it but believe it or not, crappie can be caught in muddy water. This realization became apparent when I found some crappie caught in a net in extremely muddy water that had been muddy for weeks! Their stomachs were bulging with shad which proved that they had to be feeding by sound and vibration.

Ronnie Guyton confirmed my prognosis. "I love it when the water's muddy! Fish will head for shallow cover ahead of the mudline and stay near the bank, which starts clearing up first. I'll take a tub jig (color's not important) on my Slater crappie pole and work it slowly around stumps and brush. They hit it from its vibrations."

Crappie, like other fish, will move ahead of an influx of stained water until they can go no further. However, if they are in deep water, they may elect to sink below the muddy surface layer and "suspend" until it clears. Counting down a jig or trolling is productive in this situation.

On the other hand, not all of the lake or river is likely to be muddy all over. There are usually a few tributaries that will remain clearer due to springs, current or a different type of drainage basin. Conversely, an ultra-clear condition normally found in desert lakes which is suddenly "muddied up" from a spring freshet can be a bonanza! In this latter case, seek out the area where the stained and clear water meet and be prepared to load the boat! In both cases, fishing the edge where the water is clearing is the preferred location.

Joe Rattray, a guide and campground owner on Lake Weiss, Alabama's claim to the "Crappie Capital of the World," says, "Dirty water does turn off anglers but you can still catch fish with a little extra effort. I locate structures with a depth finder and anchor alongside. It could be a treetop, brushpile or cluster of stumps on the edge of a dropoff. Fish straight down with a tightline rig on a 12-foot fiberglass pole. Use pink or orange jigs on two droppers tied at one foot intervals above a one-ounce sinker. Probe into every nook and cranny of the structure. This method covers the hideout better than by casting."

Yes, springtime is the stuff that crappie fishermen's dreams are made of and cold fronts, floods and muddy water are only temporary nightmares that can be overcome with diligent fishing. YOU GOTTA BELIEVE!

STANDING TIMBER

Acres and acres of standing timber pose an interesting question.......Where do you start? It's simple, use your depth finder to locate the migration routes (ditches, sloughs, creeks) and follow them until you start catching fish. Standing timber in lowland lakes and rivers produce best in the spring during spawning and again in the fall. Forget casting. Use a long pole or fly rod with a $\frac{1}{16}$-ounce tube jig. Swing the jig past a tree or log and let it kiss the water quietly. If nothing strikes, make another presentation, this time shallower. Still no action? Hold the jig beside the cover as motionless as possible for as long as you can stand it (a minute or two). Always fish the shady side first unless it's very early spring or late fall when they may prefer the sunny side. Start on the outside edge of the timber because the big females may be holding there waiting for ideal spawning conditions. Keep the boat in the deeper water of the channel or ditch and fish every piece of cover on each side. Make a few more presentations to a tree or stump that has some green brushy growth in the water. Also look for leaning trees or limbs that are laying at an angle in the water. Crappie like any kind of overhead protection when this shallow. Follow the route all the way to the shoreline, another prime place to prospect if there's cover. Don't think for a minute that the water's getting too shallow for big crappie—they'll spawn in water 8 inches deep! The jon boat, as it has been for decades, is the premiere craft for this kind of fishing because of its lightness, durability and shallow draft. An experienced angler with a short, sculling paddle can easily slip up on spawning crappie in the shallowest of water!

Post-Spawn Crappie

Chapter XI

After crappie have spawned and left their shallow water haunts, where do they go? For many fishermen, they might as well have left the lake. If dabbling around shoreline cover with a bobber and minnow doesn't produce a stringer of fillets, these anglers soon give up and put away the poles until next year. Perhaps this type of angler would never change his habits, but there is good reason to.

Crappie obviously haven't left the lake. They probably haven't even gone very far from the bushes or stumps they spawned in, and some still may be spawning in spite of the lateness of the season. So don't put away those poles yet.

Their first move from the bedding grounds will occur at different intervals depending on factors such as when they first arrived, water temperature, turbidity, cold fronts, and fishing pressure. Not all of them will spawn at the same time or leave the shallows at the same time. The breeding process may last into summer. Therefore, unless you're absolutely sure otherwise, it doesn't hurt to look in shallow water the first hour or two to catch late spawners. But give that up quickly if it doesn't produce any fish and then work deeper water.

Let's take a look at a typical lowland, midland and highland lake and examine what goes on with the crappie fishery in late spring and summer.

OLD HICKORY

Old Hickory near Nashville, Tennessee, is a fairly typical lowland lake. Its 22,500 acres of water are stretched in a long, narrow band up the Cumberland River Basin for 97 miles. It has a dominant river channel with flanking shallow deltas and well-defined tributaries. Completed in 1955, Old Hickory has lost all natural cover with the exception of stumprows. The Corps of Engineers and the Tennessee Wildlife Resources Agency (TWRA) have cooperated in an extensive fish attractor program resulting in the placement of brush and tire pyramids at numerous locations.

The lower end of the impoundment, below the U.S. Hwy. 231 bridge near Lebanon, is the best area for crappie because of the broader expanses of flats and larger creeks. Bledsoe, Barton's Station Camp, Spencer, Cedar, and Drake's creeks all are prime areas.

Being a lowland lake like Barkley and Toledo Bend, Old Hickory is heavily influenced by current created by power generation which causes it to rise and fall quickly, but never more than one foot a day either way. Normal pool level of 445 feet above sea level is maintained within this fluctuation throughout the year with occasional exceptions.

Discharges from two dams in the headwaters——Cordell Hull on the main stem and Center Hill on the Caney Fork River——keep Old Hickory cooler than other lowland lakes which delays the normal spawning rites of crappie and often prolongs the crappie season into June.

According to Bill Pearson, owner of Cedar Creek Marina, the springtime migration to the shallows is dependent on the influence of wind, muddy water, and cold fronts on water temperature. Weedbeds are a favorite area for the papermouths on Old Hickory. During May, and the first two weeks of June, crappie invade the weeds which actually are water willow plants. Each has a single stalk and is easy to fish around—unlike other aquatic growths which mat together in a canopy. Water willows grow on mud and gravel shorelines in one to three feet of water. Oftentimes, their location is some distance from deep water but crappie still will make the trip, especially if there's a fencerow, ditch, or rock fence leading them into the green growth.

Standard operating procedure calls for the old crappie standby—a cane pole, bobber, and minnow. Of course, modern day panfish addicts prefer hollow fiberglass poles or 8- to 10-foot fly rods fitted with a small spinning reel. Ease along the outside edge of the weedline and drop the minnow in every space available. Sometimes the water is so shallow the quill cork won't stand up and you'll have to notice it barely moving sideways. A crappie is usually on the other end. Catches in the weedbeds when the crappie are "in" can amount to 200 to 300 fish a day. (*Author's note: Tennessee has instituted a creel limit of 30 crappie, 60 in possession.*)

Brush shelters and rockpiles in less than six feet of water also produce heavy stringers at this time of year. So does the brush sunk around many of the countless boat docks. "But, only if they're mossy," Bill Pearson says. "There's something about moss on brush, rocks, and stumps that makes them more productive. New brushpiles are always better in their second year. And stumps that stay wet during lake fluctuations are producers while those that go dry are no good."

Ultralight spinning equipment and $1/16$- or $1/8$-ounce jigs in yellow or white are the medium for crappie around the rocks and woody cover. A round plastic float (run the line directly through the float rather than clipping it on the line) is attached 18 to 30 inches above the jig. Cast the rig bolo fashion beyond the target and drag it by slowly. It doesn't take much brush to hold a big school of crappie. Just a few hardwood stakes stuck in the mud often will attract a finny gathering. The old veterans who place their own brushpiles try not to expose the tips of the brush so they won't be visible to interlopers. They select an object on the shoreline to help identify its location rather than use floating markers.

By late May, in a normal year, Old Hickory crappie either move to brushpiles in deeper water or along creek channel dropoffs which have cover. Pearson says, "Don't ever fish over 15 feet deep in Old Hickory at this time of year. Usually around 10 feet is the magic depth—a depth that defeats most of the enthusiasts. They just don't want to take that cork off and fish tightline with two hooks on dropper lines above a half-ounce sinker. This method is standard around here for deep water crappie, but the extra effort required to locate fish eliminates a lot of fishing pressure."

A good depth finder is essential on lowland lakes where a meandering creek channel requires a set of underwater eyes. Start in the upper end of the tributary and work downstream until a concentration of fish is located. Outside bends with stumps or brush and the proper depth of water are a crappie fisherman's dream come true.

PERCY PRIEST

Percy Priest (also near Nashville) is a good example of a midland lake; others include Stockton and Hartwell lakes. Midland reservoirs have, as their name suggests, in-between characteristics that set them apart. Their dams are higher than lowland dams but not as high as the highland ones. The drop to winter pool is not as great as in the highland impoundments. And in their head waters, generally about halfway up from the dam, the reservoirs retain the characteristics of lowland systems by having tributaries with shallow flats and creek channel dropoffs. In other words, like offspring, they'll have traits of both parents and a few of their own.

Percy Priest's 14,200 acres are roughly divided along these lines——from the Bryant Grove Recreation Area upstream, the lake is dominated by Stewart, Spring, and Fall creeks. After spawning, crappie congregate on their dropoffs. Downstream, all the way to the dam, crappie move from spawning sites on shoreline stumps, rocks, and planted brushpiles to similar structures in 10 to 15 feet of water. Or, they "suspend" at, or near, that same depth on channel points, dropoffs and bluffs. Later in the summer, the schools will move deeper into the tops of standing timber along the Stones River channel. Otherwise, there's no visible tree cover unless one has fallen into the water along the shoreline. Fish attractors are being added by the Corps and TWRA to supplement the lack of natural cover in shallow water. These efforts seem to be working. Priest is enjoying its finest crappie fishing.

Guide Harold Morgan enjoys the results of his "Morgan Sweep" technique.

Guide Harold Morgan takes a different approach when the lake is above summer pool (490). He heads for the rocky bluffs which flank the Stones River channel at scattered intervals. Harold says, "Find a bluff with two ledges at different depths and either flip a minnow on light tackle into shallow water and come off the ledge real easy or tightline with two minnows directly below the boat on the ledges. My tightline method is a little bit different from the norm—I call it the "Morgan Sweep." I take a 6 ½- foot rod and lower my rig to the bottom toward the rear of my boat. I'll lean over and begin moving the rod tip along the surface to the front of the boat. When I've reached as far as I can, I'll come up in a sweeping motion—not straight up—kind of like drawing a "C" backward. When the fish see those minnows leaving, it makes 'em hit."

In a way, the "Morgan Sweep" is a form of slow trolling—a technique in its traditional form that is deadly on Priest crappie in the lower end of the lake. Any sloping bank or point is subject to holding scatterings of fish. Ten to 12 feet seems to be the magic depth. Troll 200 to 300 feet behind the boat with a silver and black Deep Wee R. Strangely enough, a crawfish color is good also. My personal favorite is the smaller version in the R series—the Teeny R in either of the two colors mentioned previously or the Tennessee Shad. The plug needs to be on or near the bottom, unless you've blundered into a suspended school over deep water. The presence of a graph can often turn these accidental blunderings into a sure thing on return trips.

There's only one problem with trolling plugs on gravel banks for crappie—other species of fish keep getting in the way. And it takes forever to get a big smallmouth, largemouth, or channel catfish in with 300 feet of line out.

DOUGLAS

Highland lakes perhaps are the most difficult to fish of the three types after the spawn but those such as Douglas, Bull Shoals, and Dale Hollow are full of the "silver perch" and worthy of special effort. Actually, they may be easier to fish. If crappie have left shallow water cover, they're either in fallen treetops on deep banks or they can be caught trolling.

On Douglas, a 30,400-acre TVA impoundment on the French Broad River near Knoxville, Tennessee, crappie move into the upper ends of creeks and hollows to spawn around the flooded willows. Depending on factors discussed previously, the spawn can last into May, and fish sometimes remain in the willows after spawning until June.

When they do leave, the exodus isn't far. Walter Green, owner of Swann Farm Dock near the middle of the 43-mile long impoundment, says that crappie remain in creeks such as Flat, Seehorn, Indian, and Nina all summer. Fishermen either resort to tightlining minnows in shoreline treetops and fish attractors or trolling. Jigs can be substituted for minnows if you'll use the soft plastic bodies and rig them weedless on the jighead. Charlie Brewer's weedless crappie jigs are suited ideally for this situation.

Hundreds of fish attractors have been placed in Douglas, seemingly in every cove or shoreline indention. Walter says they'll be better when they've had time to settle down and perhaps grow some moss—the same theory we heard on Old Hickory Lake. Some of the attractors are in deep water which should help concentrate fish after they've left the shoreline.

The other post-spawn alternative—trolling—is popular among Douglas devotees. The method is traditional. Two or three rods are rigged with a small, deep-diving plug on the end and two crappie jigs (chartreuse, 1/16-ounce) tied at intervals above. Trollers parallel the banks in 8 to 12 feet of water with a lot of line out. It's effective, but you have to get out there and try it first.

Don't give up when the crappie leave the shallows. Adjust your equipment and adopt a method that will produce crappie after the spawn. Believe me, they haven't left the lake!

SIGHT, SOUND & SCENT

by Bob Holmes

Chapter XII

Let's develop a three-track pattern approach to improve your crappie catching odds......**SIGHT, SOUND & SCENT**. But first of all don't forget a cardinal rule: There is no substitute for a properly presented bait (natural and artificial) in the presence of fish. No magic cure-all will bypass proper lure presentation, effective and controlled boat positioning and/or knowledge of feeding, habitat, and location preferences of crappie in your lake.

You must invest time at home reading good fishing information and studying topo maps of your fishing area. Reliable underwater reconnaissance can still be obtained by lead and line methods; however, quality flashers, paper chart recorders and Liquid Crystal Recorders are available within the budget of most fishermen.

After studying at home and obtaining a basic electronic aid, take the time to use the information and equipment on the water. Plan to devote 25% (one hour out of four) of your time to exploring, scouting or just riding around at low speed using your depth sounder to survey the lake bottom. Keep plenty of "H" shaped plastic markers to mark unusual features and schools of fish. Oftentimes, schools of fish "suspend" and won't be in or around a treetop for example, but will be relating to the structure from some distance away. Only a set of underwater eyes can locate a school in this situation.

Once you build your basic fishing knowledge and confidence, the **THREE TRACK PATTERN** will help fine tune your fishing efforts.

SIGHT

With few exceptions, most spiny-ray fish (crappie, bass, bluegill, etc.) are sight feeders. **COLORS** work! They catch thousands of fishermen every season and they catch thousands of fish too! The introduction of the **COLOR-C-LECTOR** in the mid-80s helped produce an explosion of new colors and color combinations. The **COLOR-C-LECTOR** is not a magic machine but only a guide which indicates the <u>most visible colors under current conditions</u>. During a day's fishing, take at least five readings: early morning, late morning, noon, early afternoon and late afternoon. Also take additional readings as conditions change such as the appearance or disappearance of cloud cover or the clarity of water. A fisherman may only move into the next bay or creek but runoff from the drainage basin could offer a completely different set of sight conditions.

Check the Color-C-Lector several times throughout the day because light intensities change constantly

Experiment with colors and color combinations! Develop what I called my **OFFENSIVE & DEFENSIVE STRATEGY** in a previous chapter on **PLASTIC BODIES**. Through personal experience and/or Color-C-Lector use, pick four to six initial color choices, Rig 'em and Fish 'em! If they work in 30 minutes to an hour, great. If not, cut 'em off and try something else!

SOUND

Every crappie bait displaces water and therefore sets up some type of vibration. Fish do not have external ears like humans. They receive vibrations through their internal ear and lateral line. Water current, wind, wave action, boat movement, and natural hand motions stimulate even the most inanimate lure.

There are four common jig body types: **BEETLES, TWISTER TAILS, SHAD MINNOW BODIES, and TUBE TAILS**. My guidelines for the use of these bodies are as follows: tube tails are the best all-around for the majority of fishing situations; however, the other three have their place.

BEETLES are basically elongated blobs of plastic with little built-in action. Vibrations come from water displacement by applied motion. When crappie are in a spooky, neutral or slightly negative mood, their strike zone is sometimes at the very tip of their nose! A perfectly still, stationary bait like the beetle is the ticket here.

TWISTER TAILS have a thin circular ribbon of plastic molded on the body. Applied motion causes this "ribbon" to curl from side to side seductively. Long, thick tails produce lower vibration frequencies and are more effective in dingier water than thin, short tails which produce a higher vibration frequency. Twister tails are great for fishing deep (low light) in cool water because their strong continuous vibrations make them easy for crappie to locate. The swimming tails are ideal for casting and retrieving on ultra-light spinning and spincast equipment.

SHAD MINNOW BODIES have a fish-like body with a flattened lobe on the tail which moves from side to side due to water pressure which produces low frequency vibrations. This type of body has three seasonal applications for which they are unsurpassed: after-winter shad kills; around the nests of spawning crappie; in classic fall weather of cool nights and warm days.

TUBE TAILS are basically hollow tubes of plastic closed at one end with numerous small feelers cut in the other end. These feelers vibrate very rapidly at the slightest applied motion and crappie find them hard to resist. The hollow body provides a reservoir for the injection of a fish attractant which adds even more appeal to this type of offering.

SCENT

Scents are certainly not new to fishermen. Primitive man has been using them since the dawn of time. In the fifties, sixties, and seventies, modern man

began hyping "miracle" scent products although catfishermen have known about "stink" baits forever.

My theory about scent is this: certain odors—gasoline, motor oil, human hand (L-serine), are absolutely unattractive and often repel fish. If these odors repel, then it is reasonable to assume that certain odors do attract fish.

In the early eighties, **FISH FORMULA**, an oil-based liquid fish attractant revolutionized scent technology with research, education, and proven results. In 1987, a visual component, **SPARKLSCALES**, was added. Thousands of sparkles diffuse around the bait and in the strike zone, imitating the scales knocked off of a baitfish when it is attacked—a visual strike trigger.

The sparkles also break the **FISH FORMULA** into smaller scent molecules and help disperse the scent to a wider area. Sparklscales CRAPPIE Formula was specially formulated for both white and black crappie with gold and red sparkles and should also be used on live bait as well as artificial.

I was initially very skeptical about Fish Formula but consistent use soon proved to me that Fish Formula was a very valuable addition to my crappie arsenal. I can conservatively estimate that it improves my catch anywhere from 10 to 25 percent. However, don't forget my opening statement: "There is no substitute for a properly presented bait (natural or artificial) in the presence of fish."

Crappie Tournaments

Chapter XIII

Perhaps the single thing separating the crappie fisherman from his counterpart, the bass fisherman, has been tournaments. Ray Scott started it all in 1967 on Beaver Lake in Arkansas. Stan Sloan of Tennessee won the event with a topwater lure and the fishing world hasn't been the same since. A lot of the contestants in that tournament fished out of crappie boats! But that all changed dramatically......technology has stripped its gears trying to keep the bass fisherman a step ahead of his competitor, not to mention the poor bass.

Horsepower ratings jumped on the outboards and boats had to be built to handle them. Science and engineering produced lighter, stronger and faster hulls. Joe Reeves took his Hydra-Sport hull to the Arnold Engineering Development Center's wind tunnel in Tullahoma, Tennessee to produce the most aerodynamic design on the market.

Other technological innovations came from Sonar, which each year has seemingly produced a better version of last year's model. Trolling motors, water temperature meters, ph meters, dissolved oxygen meters, and now Color-C-Lectors have made their appearance and impact.

Equipment has to be the best because livelihoods began to depend on finishing in the money! Those that were on top had great pressure on them to win because of demanding sponsors. The others that were trying to get to the top had to win consistently in order to attract a quality sponsor. It's still that way—the competition is keen because the stakes are so high.

Through all of this revolution, the crappie fisherman had pretty much remained status quo. He'd give the bass boats a good cussing when they roared by his anchored boat and stop the fish from biting temporarily. But with the exception of the trolling motor and Carl Lowrance's little green box, he didn't change much until the 80s. And I'm not sure exactly what happened then except that my first guess is that the legions of bass fishermen were getting tired of catching one or two fish a day and were burning out, while the crappie fisherman was not only catching more fish because of less pressure, he had extended his season from spring to year-round with the aid of the depth finder. Plus, the realization that it was an awful lot of fun to catch platter sized crappie on ultralight tackle, swelled the ranks dramatically.

The 1988 Crappiethon was held in Chattanooga, Tennessee, a city planning to become the National Sport Fishing Center of America.

The inevitable happened, 20 years after bass tournaments became popular, crappie tournaments finally became a reality. Tony Estes, a crappie fisherman from Decatur, Alabama conceived an idea he would call a Crappiethon to be held on several lakes throughout the Southeast. The mechanics of the Crappiethon were intricate and required a number of people working together on each lake to coordinate the event. Basically, the theme consists of retailers, bait shops, marinas, restaurants, and Chambers of Commerce sponsoring a number of fish for $25 per fish.

When a fish is caught with the tag number of the sponsor, the sponsor pays the amount to the bearer. Some of the fish carry price tags of greater sums— $50, $100, $1000, $5000, $10,000! Others carry prizes of boats, motors, and four-wheelers. If you're fishing a Crappiethon lake, you can't afford not to buy a $5 ticket that might yield thousands of dollars!

In 1986, a woman fishing off of the bank on Kentucky Lake caught a tagged fish that proved to be "Tangle-Free Tom" worth $25,000! She also happened to be using a Johnson reel who paid her an additional $10,000! The state of Kentucky was also happy to see all of that prize money!

However, Crappiethons are not tournaments in the true sense of the word, but they do sponsor a genuine crappie tournament the weekend before the Crappiethon in order to kick it off. Cash purses are awarded to the two-man team that brings in the heaviest 20-fish stringer and to several of the teams that follow. The competition is just as keen as in bass tournaments but not as structured because the teams can put in at any access on the lake. Polygraph tests keep everybody honest although fishermen have a hard time passing the polygraph test since fabrication and exaggeration are a natural part of their biological make up!

The top three teams in each of the more than 30 tournaments automatically qualify for the Crappie Classic where the really big bucks are handed out.

In June of 1988, 194 anglers from 18 states converged on Chickamauga Lake in Chattanooga, Tennessee. They came from Comanche, Iowa and Dearborn, Michigan to duel the rebels from the South for the title of World Champions. One hundred and twenty five years earlier, there had been another confrontation in the shadow of Lookout Mountain overlooking the Tennessee River......the Civil War battle at Chickamauga. Over 35,000 casualties resulted from one of the bloodiest battles of the War between the States.

Hopefully, there would be no casualties this day except for crappie. The gun smoke and cannon fire from the boys in blue and gray were replaced on this cool June morning by the roar of outboard motors as 97 teams sped away from the launching ramp a little after sun-up. Some of the smaller boats fell behind in the prop wash of the high powered engines but they weren't behind at the weigh-in. The lighter-powered boats didn't cover as much water but they covered it more methodically and were able to entice a few more fish with a careful presentation. The crappie just weren't cooperating—an unseasonable cold front slammed the door on what is otherwise an outstanding crappie-producing lake.

Chickamauga is a TVA impoundment of the Tennessee River and it has an excellent blend of creek and river channel dropoffs, bridges, bluffs, boathouses and grass beds. About 50 miles upstream, if you wanted to run that far, are the tailwaters of Watts Bar dam where some cooler, more oxygenated water could be coming through the turbines that crappie might favor.

Pickings were slim, however, and limits of 20 fish per team were rare. Both jigs and minnows were cited as having caught fish. One retired couple had qualified for the Classic by fishing off the bank! Yep, that's the way they fished in the Classic. Best friends, husbands/wives, senior citizens and women teams fished all day under the hot Tennessee sun and nobody complained......it was a great tournament and minds were set that they'd be back next year!

The winning team, Bobby Jacobs of LaCross, Virginia and Ellis Arthur of Baskerville, Virginia, had 13.01 pounds of crappie to take home, 2 fully-rigged Lowe crappie boats, cash and other prizes for a grand total of $35,000!

Tournaments are both fun and educational, maybe even rewarding. The Crappiethon Classic is the "biggie" but there are a number of others being put on by marinas, vacation resorts, fishing clubs, charities and Chambers of Commerce. If you don't win, at least learn something that may make a difference the next time out.

But don't quit your job and go on the crappie tournament circuit......unless, of course, the wife is working and the kids are out of school!

Can you imagine catching a fish worth $50,000? It'd be like winning the lottery! But it can happen in a Crappiethon if you're using the sponsor's equipment!

CRAPPIETHON USA

2ᴺᴰ BIG
FISH

484	1	PARKER HAYSLIP 94	16	
426	1	MOUNTSMAN COOMBS 58	17	

Summer

Chapter XIV

Crappie get into their "Summer" pattern well before the warm weather season actually starts. On some lakes, it may be as early as late April when the spawning migration filters back to deep water haunts. On others, it often occurs during the month of May. By the official "first" day of summer (21 June), crappie are already in their late summer pattern in deep water. Early summer patterns begin in May while crappie are schooling at medium depths in coves, bays, and tributaries off the main body of the lake. Two primary depth zones prevail in summer crappie fishing: 8 to 13 feet in early summer and 14 to 25 feet in late summer.

The return to the deep is inevitable and is performed in spite of optimum conditions that still exist in the shallows. Water temperatures are ideal, there's adequate to excessive cover, and food is plentiful. So why do they leave the shallows so soon after spawning? Well, the males don't. They stay behind to guard the nest and raise the family. It's the females who leave the home-making chores and retire to other pursuits. The same staging areas that were used during the spring migration will be used again after spawning. In no particular hurry if food and cover are present, crappie may take four to six weeks before finally arriving at their summer hangouts.

Anglers encountering water temperatures in the 70s in May and early June can expect to find crappie still in the bays and tributaries around structures in 8 to 13 feet of water. Strategically placed bushpiles are dynamite during this season and there are a lot of fish on dropoffs and breaklines.

It's the ideal time to fish—temperatures are pleasant, water levels are stable, cold fronts are memories, winds aren't as prevalent, and the crappie are aggressive.

Casting jigs, tightlining with minnows, trolling, and jig poling all produce during early summer and it merely depends on personal preference. The key is locating fish-holding structures with a good set of maps and a depth sounder.

As water temperatures start turning into the 80s, crappie head for the main lake or river channel to look for cooler water. They'll stay in this late summer holding pattern through August.

Scott Wicker of Eddyville, Kentucky is of the opinion that the stress of spawning has to be overcome by recuperation in deep water where the fish seem to be content to "suspend" for days with minimal movements. Scott says,

Boathouses offer shade and perhaps cover in the form of planted brushpiles for summer crappie.

Crappie often "suspend" in schools around and beneath permanently moored houseboats.

"There's a definite lull in activity immediately after spawning. The annual ritual appears to sap their vigor and they don't feed as hard, often preferring to 'suspend' at mid-depths in the middle of a bay. They're catchable if you work at it but they're not aggressive and it's a hit-or-miss situation. Locate a school on your LCR and fish a $\frac{1}{8}$-ounce jig by counting it down to the suspended depth. Fish it fairly fast with a steady rhythm, no need to hop or stop. Another way is to drift fish with three or four poles set at depths of 8, 10 and 12 feet. When you catch one, notice from what depth he came and adjust the other poles. They'll all be at that same depth."

Ronnie Guyton agrees, "Crappie fishing will slow down real bad for two or three weeks after the spawn. I can hardly catch a fish during this phase until they get back to deep water. By deep water, I mean from 8 to 12 feet during June. When it really gets hot, the fish move into 12 to 20 feet of water on dropoffs when there is a daily current."

Ronnie continues to use a 10-foot Slater jig pole and tube jigs for his summer style of fishing, while a great many others opt for the traditional Kentucky Lake rig to probe the dropoffs on the Tombigbee chain of lakes.

SPIDER RIGS

The move from spawning areas in shoreline vegetation is the exodus the spider riggers have been waiting for. So called for its obvious resemblance to a spider, a properly rigged spider boat can really strain open water in search of crappie.

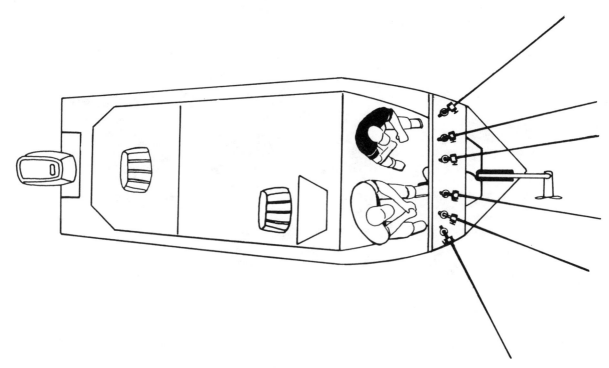

Spider rig fishing is technically a form of trolling with one notable exception......boat movement is controlled by a bow-mounted electric motor instead of a transom-mounted outboard. Other differences include two pedestal seats mounted side-by-side on the front deck behind a wooden bar which holds six to eight rod or pole holders. Sometimes a depth finder is also mounted on the bar with the transducer attached to the trolling motor.

With this arrangement, two anglers can experiment with different jig colors at various depths to quickly determine where crappie are "suspending." Buddy Boyd of Almo, Kentucky says that there's usually an 18-inch layer of water where crappie will tend to group. A jig or minnow has to be presented very close to that layer in order to catch a fish. The multiplicity of colors and depth choices of the spider rig speeds up the search significantly. However, this 18-inch layer will vary during the day and adjustments to the depth have to be made.

In early summer, when water temperatures are still changing, crappie are constantly moving in response to those changes. Biologists estimate that crappie move farther as a result of a two- or three-degree water temperature change than any other fish. Spider riggers keep up or catch up with these movements faster than other methods.

Buddy fishes eight fiberglass poles ten feet long and prefers a super limber action in the bream category. The "give" in the pole tip when a crappie hits the jig keeps him holding the bait longer without realizing that they've gotten hold of the wrong thing. Fly rods are very effective on a spider rig.

Buddy says, "I use different color jigs set at different depths on my eight poles. That way, I can estimate color and depth at the same time. The poles are rigged with only one jig. Many spider riggers use multiple (two or three) lures or minnows on each pole but I get better action and results with one jig and a #4 split shot 18 inches above it on 6-pound line. When the line hits a wave, it gives the jig a little quiver that's hard for crappie to resist!

"Jigs should be small ($1/_{16}$ or $1/_{32}$). Rarely do I go as heavy as $1/_8$ ounce. Southern Pro tube jigs are my favorite because they'll outproduce the curly tail variety. If I had to choose one color, it would be red and chartreuse with glitter. But thank goodness, I don't! I like to follow the advice of my Color-C-Lector because it will get you in the right family of colors which can save a lot of time."

The most important factor in spider rig fishing is keeping the lures straight down below the boat. Don't let them angle back toward the boat or they'll rise out of the productive zone.

In the summer, spider riggers probe along the dropoffs of deep secondary creek channels and the breaklines of underwater islands and roadbeds. As the dog days set in, crappie migrate out of the creeks to the main river channel where there is some semblance of current and cooler temperatures. Here they may lay as deep as 35 feet.

Because crappie fishermen have never had the luxury of boat manufac-turers designing a boat specifically for them, they've had to improvise and customize to suit their particular needs. Buddy Boyd, with help from Shane and Gary Darnell of Murray, Kentucky, developed their own version of a spider rig boat which sold so well to friends that Fiberking boats began producing it in their factory at Smyrna, Tennessee (See chapter on Boats).

"Spider rigs will catch crappie year round," says Buddy Boyd. "Even in the spring during spawning because they're not all in the bushes at the same time. Some of them will still be in open water on the secondary channels. However, it's in the summer when the method puts fish in the boat when others fail."

TROLLING

Although spider rigs are a form of trolling by definition, my concept of trolling extends from boyhood days of dragging a lure far behind the boat over the underwater sandbars of Mississippi River oxbow lakes and the wooded points of Bear Creek Lake in southeast Arkansas. It was and still is a very effective way to fish.

Another pre-teen experience involving trolling made a profound impression on me. I was invited to go fishing with a congenial old man whose name has eluded me but not the way he fished.

He had a large boat, about as wide as it was long, with a whopper of a motor for those days—10 Horsepower! The craft sported a roof and rod holders across the front and down both sides. Two big bundles of cane poles were tied on either side of the roof which appeared to be a tangle of hooks and lines that would be hard to unravel. I was wrong. We hadn't idled very far from his dock on Moon Lake in North Mississippi when all 12 of the poles were vibrating in their holders.

Each pole was equipped with either three minnows or three Hot-Shots tied at two foot intervals on the nylon line (monofilament hadn't been invented) along with a lead weight. We proceeded down the lake, comfortably seated in the big boat and proud of the top that was keeping the hot summer sun from baking our tender skin.

I had almost forgotten why we were there when three of the poles on the bow and one on the right side started dancing and dipping their tips into the water from struggling crappie. The old man fumbled with a marker to throw out while I attempted to handle one of the long cane poles.

Pandemonium had the upper hand there for a few minutes until we finally got things in order and resumed our trolling run. This time we had the school marked and were ready for action. Pandemonium again took over.

Oh, those were the days! Alas, poor Moon Lake, once full of gamefish, is now on the endangered list and doesn't provide the largess she once did. But others do and places like Tunica Cutoff, Brandywine, Midway, Whitehall, and Cold Creek still produce coolers of summer crappie caught by trolling.

Trolling will produce crappie the major part of the year in any water where they are present in good numbers—from the 10,000 lakes of Minnesota to the canyon impoundments of Arizona.

Skill, coordination and on-the-water experience are required for successful "spider-rig" fishing.

OXBOWS

The trolling techniques that I first experienced in the 50s are still in vogue today up and down the Mississippi River Valley.

Jim Fowler of Tunica, Mississippi has been trolling an old oxbow by the name of Tunica Cutoff since the early 60s. He liked the former river-run lake so much that he now resides year-round at the Nel-Win Camp. His trailer sits high off the ground on pilings because "Ole Miss" tends to get out into the bottoms every spring.

When the river's up and reads over 12 feet on the Memphis gauge, water is in the trees and the crappie soon follow. Keep an eye on the river stage readings in the daily paper and when it drops to 10 feet or below, it's time to troll because falling water levels have drawn the crappie out of the woods and into open water. Other oxbows will have a different gauge reading that signals the water is out of the trees and experience is the best teacher to tell you whether the crappie will be in the cover or "suspended" in open water.

Oxbows are all basically the same—they're either C-shaped or backward C-shape depending on which side of the river was cut off. Usually the outside bend of the C is the area of deepest water in the oxbow. The inside bend will be shallower and floods easily when the river rises. (See oxbow diagram Chapter 1.)

Jim Fowler started trolling in a 14-foot jon boat with four poles, corks and small lead weights. Minnows were hooked through the dorsal fin. He soon advanced to six poles, each with three dropper hooks tied to a three-way swivel. Minnows were hooked through the eyes. Instead of a small lead sinker, Jim began using one of 6 ounces!

Each method worked but Jim was constantly striving to fine-tune his method. That led him into a bigger boat (16 foot) from which he could fish 14 poles—10 across the front and 2 on each side. An 8-ounce weight was added to keep the lines from going back too far in the water. The terminal rig remained the same—three hooks on each line baited with minnows. Results were astonishing......as many as 200 to 300 fish a day were often caught. It took three people to man the operation—two taking fish off and rebaiting while the third ran the boat.

The hard work under a broiling sun necessitated another change—a more comfortable boat. Jim bought a 28-foot pontoon boat with two motors—a 70 hp to get to the trolling area and a 6 hp to do the trolling. Jim says, "Troll 2 to 5 mph; anything over that gets the lines more than 45° back. If the speed is too slow, the lines hang straight down and won't catch."

His new pontoon is outfitted with 18 poles of a type he's always used. It's the one thing he hasn't changed—20-foot Sweetheart canes imported from Japan! A heavy (20- to 30-pound test) line is used to keep from tearing up the rig when he runs through a school of 3-ounce white bass! Gars also pose a threat.

"I was working too hard rebaiting hooks and keeping minnows alive," says Jim. "I had to switch to jigs. At first I tried $1/32$- and $1/64$-ounce sizes but the hook was too small to get the fish in sometimes so I settled on $1/16$- and $1/8$-ounce Canyon tube jigs. The jigs allowed me to add two more drops to each pole and many times three crappie are caught on the same pole, sometimes four!

"On sunny days, the bottom lures catch the fish and on cloudy days, the top lures have their turn. Until late summer, crappie are generally suspended in water 10 to 15 feet deep. They don't seem to relate to any kind of structure but they will stay in the same general area for quite some time and return to that area year after year.

"When the water gets real hot, the fish move out over deeper water (20-45 feet) but still "suspend" about 12 to 15 feet. The only way to keep track of a suspended school is by landmarks on the bank. They won't be far from where you last left them."

MIDLAND LAKES

Trolling is the best method to catch crappie in the summer on midland types of lakes. The fish are deep, but not as deep as you might expect. Water clarity, weather, water temperature, and dissolved oxygen all play a part in determining the whereabouts of the local gangs of crappie. Trolling is the quickest way to make these determinations, especially on a strange lake. Concentrate your efforts on the one-third of the lake nearest the dam where the deepest water prevails but think in terms of a 13- to 25-foot zone. This same zone will also prevail in other types of lakes and is a good rule of thumb to follow in the summer.

Crappie Guide Harold Morgan has developed his own brand of trolling on Percy Priest. Although Priest has a certain amount of inundated standing timber along the old Stones River channel which does harbor crappie, Harold prefers drift fishing aided by a bow-mounted trolling motor.

His tackle consists of six-foot and seven-foot spinning rods outfitted with identical Kentucky Lake tightline rigs. The rods are fished side by side and the different lengths keep them from tangling with each other.

Harold offers this opinion, "When fish are suspended off the bottom, spread the dropper hooks wider and higher on the line for better catching power. Otherwise, you'll be fishing under them and the concensus among the experts is a crappie will come up for a minnow but won't go down. On the other hand, sometimes they're hugging the bottom after a front and you have to move the hooks down to about 10 inches apart to keep from going over them."

Until he finds a definite pattern, Harold rigs one rod with minnows and one with white and chartreuse curly tail jigs in either $1/16$- or $1/8$- ounce sizes depending on the wind. On real windy days, he adds a split shot above the jigs for weight and better line control. Being from the old school of crappie fishing, Harold voices a decided preference for lively minnows. "I like small minnows—they pay off better on this midland lake than the bigger ones."

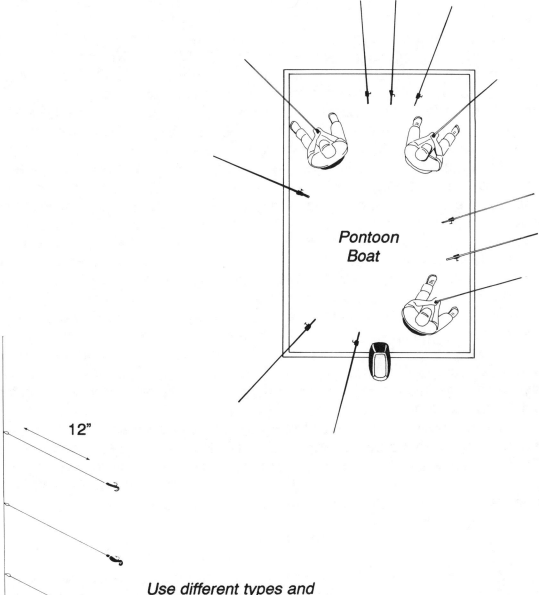

Pontoon
Boat

12"

Use different types and
colors of jigs.

12"

The Fowler Rig

Harold first prospects for summer crappie "on the plains." The "plains" are huge flat areas near the river channel. With his flasher unit, he seeks any kind of break in the bottom—a shallow ditch, high spot, ridge, or an old house foundation.

According to the guide who gives a customer another day of fishing if he doesn't produce fish, but who rarely has to, Harold says, "Normally I'll let out 50 to 75 feet of line behind the boat directly over the breakline. On windy days, I fish even farther back. The distance varies and you have to experiment. Every little bit I'll hit the trolling motor up a notch to bring the lures toward the surface. When I slow down, they fall back. You're moving all the time, never anchor. The best times to troll this way are on windy days between 11 a.m. and 4 p.m."

Jerry Patterson also plies his trade on Percy Priest but he employs a more traditional form of trolling. He runs a small crankbait 150 to 200 feet behind the boat powered by an outboard that can get down and crawl. "The slower the motor runs, the better," says Jerry. "But, I'm all the time speeding up just enough to change the vibration of the crankbait. They'll usually hit it either on the speed up or when I slow down and it falls back. Another tactic to change the rhythm of the lure is to suddenly 'sweep' the rod forward and let it go back."

Jerry looks for suspended fish in water at least 25 feet deep. The object of his search, much like Harold Morgan's, is an irregular feature of the bottom and his favorite is a hump with a crappie convention just above it. He trolls a lure designed for bass, a Deep Wee R by Rebel. It nevertheless produces the numbers of crappie that satisfy Jerry. A variation of the rig involves a 3-way swivel with the Deep Wee R on the bottom a $1/8$-ounce pink Roostertail on top. If only those dang smallmouths would leave it alone!

My favorite lure when I was trolling the rocky shorelines of Percy Priest, and one shown to me by an expert troller, Mr. Boyd Longyear, is a Teeny R by Rebel. Strange as it may seem, the crawfish color was tops, followed by chrome with a black back. To get deeper, I often added one of Gapen's bait walkers which also allowed me to troll with less line out.

HIGHLAND LAKES

With the exception of lantern fishing, trolling may be the only way to consistently catch crappie in the deep clear impoundments in the summertime. It is definitely the best way to locate a school which can then be cast to by counting down a jig or by drifting through them with a number of poles baited with live minnows. Because of the water clarity, fishermen troll as far behind the boat as possible and the method has become known simply as long-line trolling! Some use a transom mounted trolling motor for locomotion and others opt for a small outboard.

The number of lines that can be effectively trolled depends on the experience of the angler and how hard he wants to work. Beginners should

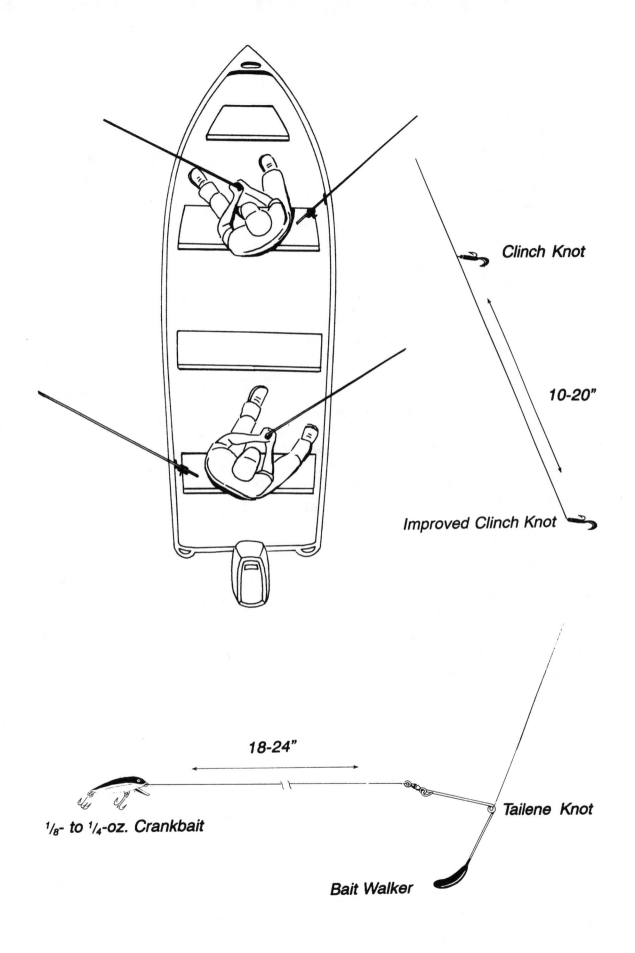

Clinch Knot

10-20"

Improved Clinch Knot

18-24"

1/8- to 1/4-oz. Crankbait

Tailene Knot

Bait Walker

start with no more than two rods per person and I have found that three rods for two people is adequate to prevent lines from tangling in turns.

A few experts can handle four or even five rods because they've set their boat up to do so. Once a troller has his boat the way he wants it, he's extremely reluctant to trade it in for a newer model and it may have antique value before he trades!

Favorite trolling boats on highland lakes are usually aluminum types with deep V-hulls to handle the rough, open waters. Until recently, trollers had to customize their own boats to suit their trolling needs but Fisher Marine has designed and is now manufacturing a deep-V model which already has rod holders in place on the rear and sides of the boat to accommodate trollers.

East Tennessee's chain of lakes are especially suited for trolling, which actually begins as early as April. Steve Carpenter of Louisville, Tennessee, runs a guide service on two of the lakes, Ft. Loudown and Tellico, when he's not writing outdoor columns for the Maryville/Alcoa *Daily Times*.

Steve starts his trolling runs on clay and gravel points in the upper ends of the lakes but moves progressively toward the dams as summer continues. He ties two $1/16$- ounce jigs about 18 inches apart on 6-pound line which runs about 10 feet deep, 150 feet behind the boat. As the heat takes its toll and the fish sink deeper, Steve either adds lead above the jigs for additional depth or he goes to a deep-diving Humpback Rebel which he can get down to 15 feet on a long line. Extra weight or a bait walker takes it down even further.

Other highlanders use the same principle of adding weight, increasing the distance behind the boat and small diameter line to get to the fish holding zone but they do it with more than one rod. A veteran troller can master as many as five rods with one rod holder on each side, another on each back corner of the boat and the fifth (rod) is held by hand.

A five-rod spread eliminates tight turns unless the two rods on the inside of the turn are reeled in. Tight turns are the exception, however, rather than the rule on most highland lakes.

These trolling tactics will take crappie in all highland lakes because they're usually not going to be deeper than can be reached by long-line trolling. If they are, there's only one alternative......get the lanterns out and fish after dark!

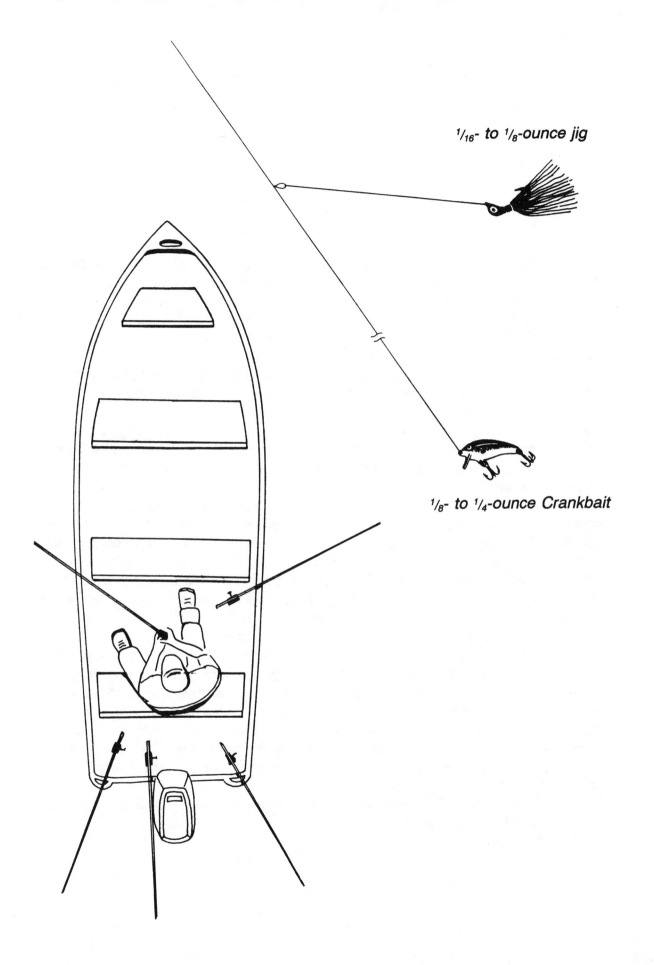

¹/₁₆- to ¹/₈-ounce jig

¹/₈- to ¹/₄-ounce Crankbait

Night Time

Chapter XV

In the summer, night time is the right time to catch a stringer of crappie. In fact, there may be no other way and you don't have to risk heat stroke.

The scheme is very basic and applies to all types of natural lakes, rivers and impoundments. A possible exception to this rule are the oxbows along the Mississippi River. Unless there's a pier or boathouse to fish from, the clouds of insect life over the water inhibit boating after dark.

On the other hand, a cloud of insects is what anglers along the Tennessee and Cumberland Rivers look for—Mayflies! Every eight to ten days during the summer, mayflies emerge from their watery womb and crappie gorge on the hapless insects. Spend a night under the lights during a major mayfly hatch and your boat will never be the same again! They'll stack up in corners you didn't know your boat had and will continue to show up in every odd place for weeks thereafter!

But I love 'em! And so do the fish! Not only crappie but every other species that swims tries to cash in on the bonanza. Locate a shoreline where a hatch is emerging just before dark and catch a bagful for bait. It takes a bunch of the big winged, light bodies to bait one hook. Jim DeVillez of Kuttawa, Kentucky demonstrated his Mayfly catching technique one evening on Lake Barkley. Jim would take a small size garbage pail liner and sneak up on a bush whose limbs were drooping from the weight of mayflies. With a lunge and a whoop, Jim encased as many as a hundred at a time!

If mayflies aren't hatching or aren't native to your part of the country, then there's a plethora, maybe even a myriad, of other insect types that will flog your lantern. Always have a least one lantern; most people have two or three tied at each end and in the middle of the boat. All on the same side. If one lantern is put on one side of the boat and another on the other side, the transfer of insects from one light to the other usually overwhelms the fisherman. Supplement (not substitute) the lanterns with one or two floating sealed beam lights which project deeper into the water.

Remember the 3 B's when looking for nighttime crappie structure—Bluffs, Bridges, and Boathouses. They can all be found on the same lake but usually one predominates.

Bluffs

At Toledo Bend, Bill Miller, III of Monroe, Louisiana, reports about a favorite area for a fleet of what he calls "Party boats" in the "Chicken Coops." Seems there's a big bluff on the Texas side of the Sabine River and on top of the bluff are its namesake—a Texas farmer's chicken coops.

Actually I know why Bill Miller, III calls them "party boats." Nighttime crappie fishing is a social occasion, a festive affair that very nearly demands mixed company, hearty food, and good drink. Other boats (practically always pontoon boats) join in and pretty soon the night belongs to Michelob!

When fishing bluffs, anchor perpendicular to the bluff itself. This not only keeps the boat from banging against jagged rocks but it is in a better position for everybody to catch fish when the activity begins. Of course this calls for a long line of at least 150 feet on the anchors and the boat is anchored at both ends. Although you may be anchored in 100 feet of water, crappie will usually be caught 20 to 30 feet deep—just below the influence of the light cast by a floating sealed beam or a lantern.

Bridges

Bridges are a favorite summer hangout for crappie. They provide everything a crappie needs—food, cover, and comfort. Plankton collect on the pilings which attract minnows which attract crappie. Although some bridges may appear to be sterile, they aren't! During the day, schools of crappie loaf in a comfort zone in the shade of the bridge, moving with the shade throughout the day. At night they move to the lights of bridge fishermen!

Not all bridges produce crappie in the summer. Only those on the main river channel or major active tributaries have the ingredients to sustain a summer fishery. Current is the prime factor—bridge construction constricts the waterway and forces water through a smaller opening. This not only creates more oxygenated water but it funnels baitfish past hungry crappie.

Bridge fishermen have one great advantage over bluff fishermen—they don't have to anchor unless there's absolutely no way to tie to the bridge. That's usually not a problem but it can be. Most bridge abutments will have a cable, rope, or nail put there by previous fishermen. Tie both ends of the boat and be sure to carry at least two boat fenders to prevent scraping and scratching.

Try to get to the bridge before dark for two reasons: (1) To get a place to fish. When the fish are hitting under the bridges, all those "party boats" won't be on the bluffs. (2) Not all bridge pilings and abutments are the same. If you've ever sat across from another piling and watched crappie after crappie being hauled over the side by your neighbor, then you know what I mean. And wouldn't you think that they would at least do it quietly? Nooo, they have to shriek, scream, and squeal each time the process is repeated! And then some kid asks throughout the night, "Are y'all catching any yet?"

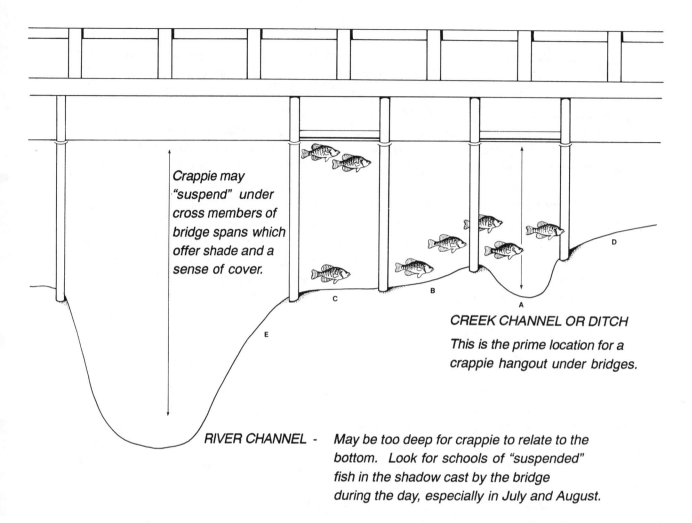

Crappie may "suspend" under cross members of bridge spans which offer shade and a sense of cover.

CREEK CHANNEL OR DITCH
This is the prime location for a crappie hangout under bridges.

RIVER CHANNEL - *May be too deep for crappie to relate to the bottom. Look for schools of "suspended" fish in the shadow cast by the bridge during the day, especially in July and August.*

So if you're not sure which piling is the hotspot, canvas up and down the bridge before dark with your depth sounder and look for ditches, rockpiles, creeks or bottom changes created during the bridge's construction. Any one of these running under the bridge is a likely thoroughfare for nocturnal travelers. Of course the main channel is a possibility but if a secondary channel or structure can be found, chances are that it will produce more fish.

Like all other forms of fishing, experience is the best teacher.

Boathouses

Boathouses are by far the easiest to fish of the three B's. You don't even have to have a boat if you have a good friend who will let you fish off his pier. Usually a pier is associated with a boathouse unless it's anchored on a bluff. The shallower the lake, the longer the pier will be to the boathouse. These are fixed, permanent piers which are made by driving pilings into the soft lake bottom for support of the walkway to the boathouse.

On certain river systems such as the Cumberland in Tennessee and Kentucky, the managing federal agency (Corps of Engineers) does not permit the installation of fixed piers. All docks have to be floating to allow for water level fluctuations and can extend no more than 50 feet from the shoreline.

Those docks will produce fish if they extend over a creek or river channel bend. The same is true of the boathouse at the end of a long pier. Only during the spring and again in the fall is the shallow water part of the pier going to hold crappie. In the summer, they'll be under the end of the pier and boathouse where the water depth changes. It's a reliable key. Fish the boathouses on the dropoff of a channel and leave the ones on the flats and in the shallow coves alone.

Fishing piers is an excellent summer pattern but chose those near a breakline for best results.

Look for the boathouses that already have a light on them and other telltale signs such as rod holders and fish cleaning stations. If these conditions are present, you can bet the egg money there will be some sort of fish attracting cover around the perimeter.

Do all prospecting before dark and be in position with a game plan for the night. Select an alternate site or sites in case of a change in plans.

When fishing the three B's at night, forget about the nuances that control daytime fishing—light line, size of jig, Color-C-Lector, graphite rods, LCR's, trolling motor, etc. Nighttime angling is very basic—any kind of tackle will do the job but I do recommend "yellow" line for its line-watching potential. Corks are rarely used unless they are of the sliding variety which can be fished deep.

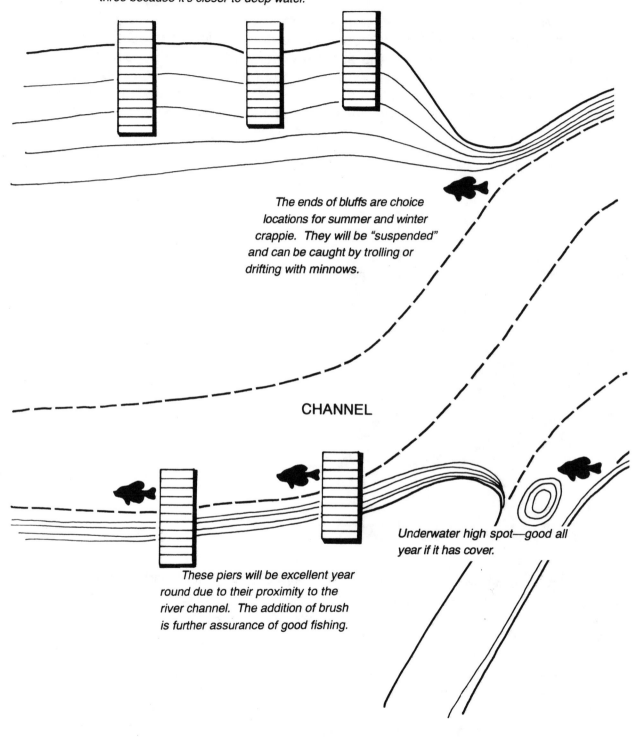

These piers aren't as good for fishing at night as those across the lake. They will hold fish in early spring and again in the fall. Pier A should be the better of the three because it's closer to deep water.

The ends of bluffs are choice locations for summer and winter crappie. They will be "suspended" and can be caught by trolling or drifting with minnows.

CHANNEL

These piers will be excellent year round due to their proximity to the river channel. The addition of brush is further assurance of good fishing.

Underwater high spot—good all year if it has cover.

Fallen trees or ledges with brush will hold crappie on bluffs. Also look for deposits of clay and gravel that have sluffed off from between rock formations.

BLUFF

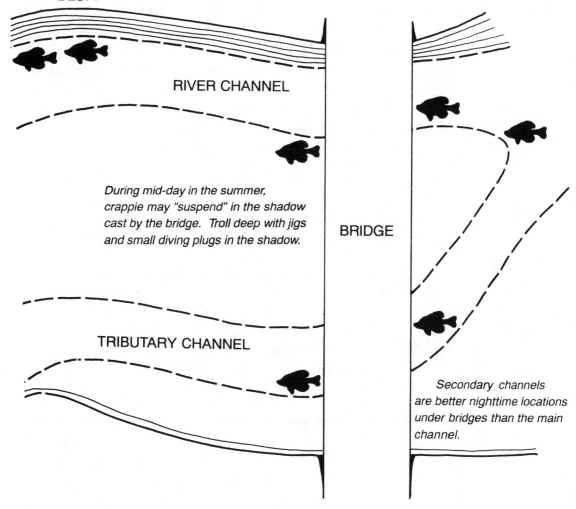

RIVER CHANNEL

During mid-day in the summer, crappie may "suspend" in the shadow cast by the bridge. Troll deep with jigs and small diving plugs in the shadow.

BRIDGE

TRIBUTARY CHANNEL

Secondary channels are better nighttime locations under bridges than the main channel.

Boats are even more basic and may include everything from a skiff to a scow. One of the worthwhile considerations is the bigger the better. Nocturnal enthusiasts generally sit in one spot for most of the night and a boat big enough to walk around in is a big plus. In addition, they have the space to carry cots, coolers and a grill. Whatever the craft, make sure it has working navigation lights and a marine compass, which is invaluable when the fog rolls in on a big lake. Fog disorients the ablest of water-wise veterans......even the Old Guide himself!

Equipment specific to the nighttime angler consists of lanterns, lights, and batteries. The venerable Coleman lantern is still the standard of the after-dark crowd. Have at least two, depending on the size of the boat, and work them in conjunction with floating sealed beams. The lanterns are better at drawing insects and sealed beams are better for attracting minnows and crappie.

Some fishermen rig up two or three clip-on lights instead of Coleman lanterns. They'll work fine once adapted to their power source but there's something about AC/DC and the light bulb that requires attention. Both types of lights work off car batteries, the weakest link in the chain. I don't think I've ever been out at night when the batteries didn't start to lose their power about the time the fish started to bite! You just can't have too many batteries, nor can they be too hotly charged for an all night vigil.

Another light that is indispensable is a high candlepower Q beam. Now this type of light will drain a battery fast so only use it sparingly when navigating to locate buoys and obstructions or to warn another boat which appears intent on running across your bow! And don't lay it on the seat while still on—it will have made a nice round hole by the time you smell the smoke!

Let me close with this final bit of information on the Right time for Nighttime—the darker the night, the better the fishing. A bright moon seems to disperse the schools of boatfish and they don't come to the lanterns as well.

Summer fishing, as with other seasons, can be broken down into early and late periods. Early summer is a time of plenty and availability. Late summer is different. Crappie are harder to find and harder to catch. However, when you do find a concentration of fish, they tend to remain in that general area throughout the hot weather season and consistent catches can be made.

Fish a pier with lights on it more carefully than one without lights. Lights may indicate the presence of brushpiles or other fish attractors since the pier's owner is obviously a fisherman.

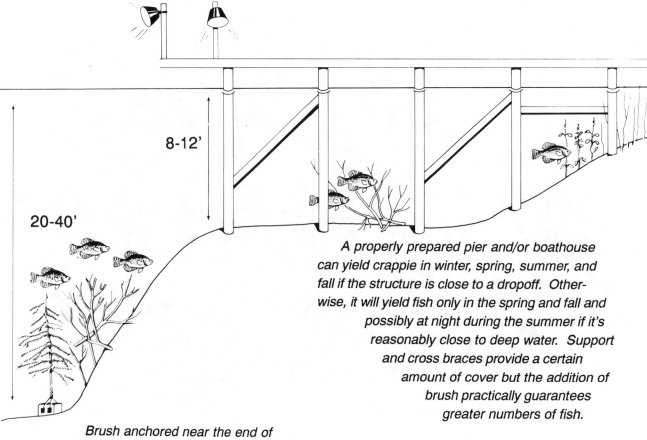

Lights projecting into the water draw
crappie at night for summer anglers.

8-12'

20-40'

A properly prepared pier and/or boathouse
can yield crappie in winter, spring, summer, and
fall if the structure is close to a dropoff. Otherwise, it will yield fish only in the spring and fall and
possibly at night during the summer if it's
reasonably close to deep water. Support
and cross braces provide a certain
amount of cover but the addition of
brush practically guarantees
greater numbers of fish.

Brush anchored near the end of
a pier on a depth change may hold
fish all year if it's deep enough.

PIER AND BOATHOUSE STRATEGY

Photo courtesy of B & M Pole Co.

Grass Crappie

Chapter XVI

The natural aging and subsequent water clarity of many of our nation's reservoirs has prompted groups of aquatic plants to invade and literally take over vast areas of heretofore open water.

Of course, water-borne vegetation is nothing new to swamps, bayous and shallow natural lakes but it is in lakes such as Alabama's Wheeler and Guntersville; Tennessee's Watts Bar and Chickamauga; and Kentucky Lake, which spans Tennessee and Kentucky.

There are many different kinds of aquatic plants and they grow in various depths of water. Hydrilla flourishes in deeper water than the other types and thus becomes a more noxious pest because it clogs navigation channels that are left open by shallow-water oriented species such as lily pads, reeds, coontail moss, Eurasian milfoil, and water willow.

Eurasian milfoil will cover shallow bays out to a depth of six to eight feet and then stop. Where it stops is the place to start crappie fishing. With one exception that I'll cover later, always fish the edges of a weedline or pockets in the weedline.

During the spring, crappie often spawn in, under, or close to some type of water vegetation. In many cases, it's the only cover available.

One of the most productive techniques for taking these papermouths is to troll along the edges of the grass with either minnows or jigs using 10- to 12-foot lightweight poles. Use a spider rig or a small (under 10 hp) outboard to troll with.

However, remember that not all crappie will be moving into the grass to spawn at the same time. There may be as many holding in deeper water as there are in the grass. So smart crappie fishermen set out several poles on the deep side as well as the opposite side when trolling a weedline.

Another place to look for crappie is in the middle of grassbeds where there are holes that an angler can swing his bait into; which allows him to catch fish that aren't available on the edge. If there aren't any holes, create some with a garden rake. Clear out ten to twelve holes in the grass and by the time you get back to the first hole to start fishing, you should be able to catch crappie. This technique is popular in the Santee-Cooper country and numerous Florida lakes.

Yet another area to look for crappie is an isolated patch of grass well away from the bank. These little islands of grass may be hosting a whole reunion of fish either spawning or getting ready to go to the bank to spawn!

Kentucky Lake guide Malcolm Lane has had to adapt his fishing and guiding tactics to help clients catch fish in this new medium. Malcolm suggests using a light sliding cork and a tube jig on ultra-light spinning gear. Cast the jig to the edge of the grassline or around isolated clumps. The sliding cork is stopped by a rubber band about a foot above the jig. Pull the jig up to the cork and let it fall back as you retrieve slowly to the boat.

The cork allows those less accustomed to casting and working a jig to keep the lure in a strike zone longer and with less chance of hanging up.

As water over the grass gets deeper, lengthen the distance between the jig and the cork stopper in order to keep the bait just above the grass tips.

Although spring is prime time for crappie in the grass, they may have to stay in it all year if the lake is shallow all over. Otherwise, after spawning they'll head for deep water dropoffs and humps for the summer.

Surprisingly, crappie return to these grass fields in the fall and stay until extremely cold weather forces them back to deeper water.

Harold Thompson of Decatur, Alabama follows a ditch or old creek channel into a bay or flat on Wheeler Lake in northern Alabama. Wheeler is primarily saturated with Eurasian milfoil which has covered entire coves, pockets and bays. Harold follows the edge of a weedline and fishes openings and clumps with a 12-foot B & M pole and drops a tuffy minnow into every likely cranny with a bobber set 12 to 18 inches deep!

Because of the water clarity, a super cautious approach is necessary to get within range. However, line size and minnow size doesn't seem to make a difference because Harold uses 12- to 20-pound test and whatever size minnows are available at the bait shop.

Why are crappie in shallow grass in late fall and on through the winter if it's relatively mild? It's simple—they're feeding!

Aquatic vegetation in all of its forms is good news and bad news. The good news is that it improves crappie fishing by providing vital cover in the crucial first year, the same as it does for bass. Grass also makes adult crappie less susceptible to angling pressure during spawning season.

The bad news is the dominance that some species such as milfoil and hydrilla can exert over a wide body of water which limits other types of pleasure boating such as water skiing and yachting. (I know, this could fall under the category of good news!) Blankets of vegetation also make lakefront property owners livid with rage every summer weekend, who then put great pressure on the local authorities to initiate control measures.

Unfortunately or fortunately, depending on your politics, an effective eradication method hasn't been found short of draining the lake dry and refilling it several months later! Since that's not likely to happen in most reservoirs, the only solution is to learn how to fish grass.

Grass can be exasperating to fish and adjustments have to be made in order to be successful.

Fall

Chapter XVII

By the end of summer, I think crappie are as anxious to get August over with as the fishermen. August can be tough and just too hot to enjoy fishing unless it's done at night or by trolling from a covered pontoon boat.

September can also be uncomfortably warm but the days are getting shorter and usually around the first week, a cold front comes through. It's the front feared by all dove hunters who are waiting anxiously on a field teeming with gray darters before the season opener. Although the untimely cold front puts doves on the move, it fortuitously wakes up summer crappie. A few cool nights is all it takes to stir crappie into movements reminiscent of spring. Although we discussed in detail the four seasons and even broke these down into early and late periods, crappie fishing can almost be lumped into two! This is because summer and winter locations are similar and spring and fall migrations are practically the same.

The primary difference in the fall migration is that there's less shoreline cover to migrate into because most reservoirs are drawn down to provide storage space for winter floods. Truman Lake in Missouri is the only man-made impoundment that I know of that gets higher in the fall by design.

Of course, natural lakes don't suffer this fate if rains materialize. Otherwise, their level remains essentially stationary. Fall crappie migration in natural lakes takes place along the same routes as spring except that they relate more to woody cover (trees, stumps, duckblinds, stakebeds, logs, and brush) than to aquatic vegetation.

Duck blinds are the most obvious structure on natural lakes for fishermen unfamiliar with the territory. The blinds are usually large affairs because they are permanent and duck hunters tend to add to them every year. Some are floating but the majority are on pilings driven into the lake bottom and constructed with plywood and 2 x 4s and covered with brush which extends into the water. They are perfect hideouts for fall crappie but make sure they're not occupied by duck hunters who may be using them in September during the early wood duck and teal seasons and again around Thanksgiving through December in the South.

In northern states, duck seasons come in earlier so be aware of the local seasons governing your state. If a mistake is made, the blind's occupants will let you know right away if you can crappie fish around their blind!

Blinds are best fished with a long pole and tube jigs. You'll only need a few feet of line because crappie will be shallow and the short line enables you to probe into every nook and cranny. Use a pole with a reel and line guides in order to grasp the line and pull the jig up to the tip so that it can be inserted into a small opening then released to fall into a waiting mouth. Don't grab the blind while doing this—they are favorite places for irritable cottonmouths, which of course won't be a problem north of Cairo, Illinois in the Mississippi River Valley.

Oftentimes, boat trails cut by duck hunters to these blinds will also hold crappie. Fish these carefully as you approach the blind, especially any kind of log, brushpile, beaverhouse, or stump along the way.

Other trails of interest to the fall crappie enthusiast are those created by beavers, muskrats and alligators. Any of them is subject to holding a number of crappie in the fall. Jigs and long poles are preferred on the trails as well as around the blinds.

A few lakes, such as Iowa's Rathbun Lake, the Tenn/Tom Waterway, and Tennessee's Old Hickory Lake maintain their level, or nearly so, in the fall months but others get lower in proportion to their storage capacity. Lowland impoundments fluctuate three to five feet from summer to winter pools; midlands anywhere from 10 to 20 feet and highlands may drop over 50 feet! Reservoirs built specifically for flood control such as Mississippi's Sardis, Grenada, Enid, and Arkabutla, also have drastic drawdowns although they are in flat land. These lakes are drained back into the original riverbed and creeks which leaves launching ramps high and dry and access difficult. Biologists are now finding greater stress levels in fish concentrated in such confined spaces.

Fall migrations start after the first cold front in September. After leaving the main channel, crappie follow the same routes as they do in spring. Their first stop or staging area is the junction of a creek, slough, or ditch; a cluster of stumps; mid-depth fish attractors; or an old roadbed. They'll remain in these types of areas until cooler temperatures push them shallower......into brush piles, downed timber, grassbeds, and shoreline vegetation that hasn't been exposed by falling water levels. Most reservoirs draw their level down in the winter which leaves most of the cover that was under-water in the spring and summer high and dry!

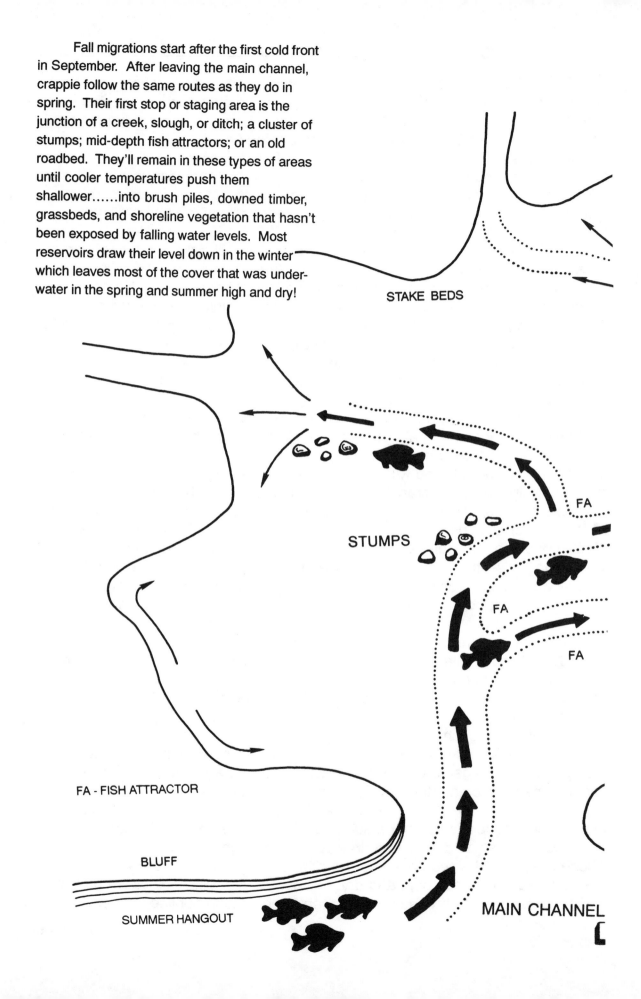

STAKE BEDS

STUMPS

FA

FA

FA

FA - FISH ATTRACTOR

BLUFF

SUMMER HANGOUT

MAIN CHANNEL

FALL MIGRATIONS

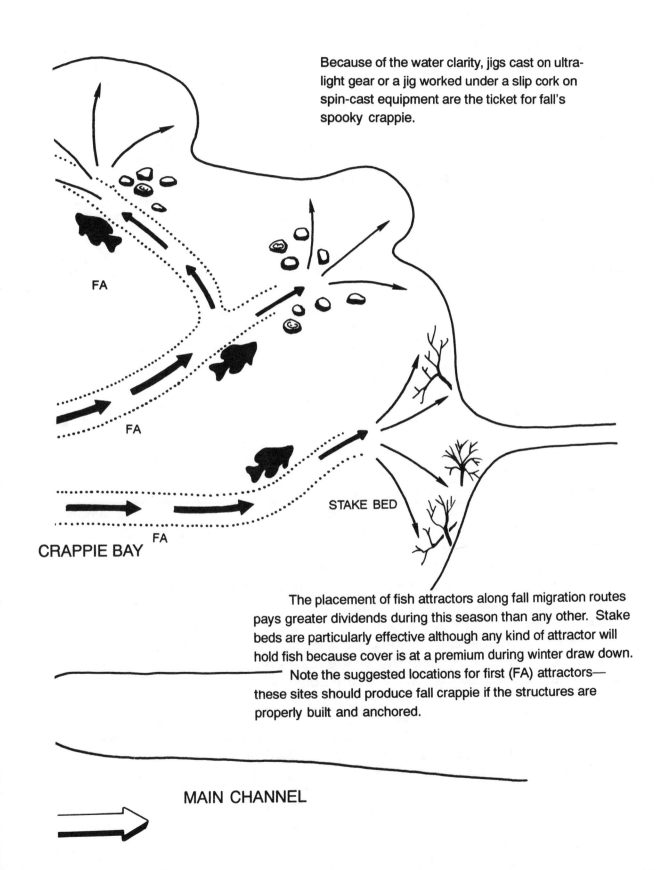

Because of the water clarity, jigs cast on ultra-light gear or a jig worked under a slip cork on spin-cast equipment are the ticket for fall's spooky crappie.

FA

FA

FA

CRAPPIE BAY

STAKE BED

The placement of fish attractors along fall migration routes pays greater dividends during this season than any other. Stake beds are particularly effective although any kind of attractor will hold fish because cover is at a premium during winter draw down. Note the suggested locations for first (FA) attractors— these sites should produce fall crappie if the structures are properly built and anchored.

MAIN CHANNEL

Lakes in the Tennessee River Valley begin their fall drawdown in July—a policy developed by the Tennessee Valley Authority that affects other water-oriented recreation as well as fishing and thought should be given to maintaining summer pool through Labor Day.

Because the fall drawdown removes a high percentage of crappie hide-outs, the isolated patches of cover that remain in the water attract and hold larger numbers of fish for a couple of months. These patches of cover may be natural (stumps, high spots, dropoffs, channel junctions) or manmade (tires, stakebeds, brush, riprap, roadbeds). Natural cover will suffice until fishing pressure dictates the addition of fish attractors known only to the builder! Attractors with five to eight feet of water over them at drawdown levels are prime fall magnets. Crappie may locate on these attractors by early September and stay until very cold weather. In the spring, these same attractors will serve as the last staging area before deploying into the shallows and the first stop after spawning.

So these attractors do yeoman service in both seasons and are vitally important to the year's success. Location of the attractors is not as critical as deep water attractors. They should be as far back in the bay or creek as water depths permit and can be scattered over a large flat area.

With the exception of river bottom lakes, water is extremely clear in the fall due to the cessation of summer's algal blooms and the lack of rainfall, which dictates a careful approach and long distance casting. Normally, you can't get within reach of a long pole or fly rod without notifying the fish.

Now is the time for a bobber and minnow delicately presented on spin casting or ultra-light spinning equipment. Cast the bobber and minnow well beyond the fish holding structure and pull it into or beside the cover. Let it sit for several minutes until something happens. A slight wind on your back allows better control of the bobber in the strike zone and makes it easier to hold near the attractor. The minnow or jig can be worked up and down in place without drifting away. Fall crappie in clear water often requires a lot of encouragement.

For casting to shallow brush, I prefer a 2-inch shad body on a $1/16$-ounce jighead (unpainted). Charlie Brewer's crappie grubs, which have a similar club-shaped tail, are also top notch. This type of tail seems to ride "up" in the water a little quicker than twister tails and I prefer the "feel" of it over tube tails. The "riding up" feature keeps it from hanging up so readily. Add one of Charlie's weedless jigheads and this problem can almost be eliminated.

Not all fall crappie choose to concentrate in shallow water—many stay on dropoffs or remain "suspended" but for the most part (about as conclusive as you can get for crappie) they will be in the uppermost one-third of the tributary of back of the bay.

Productive dropoffs will have five feet of water on top of the drop and deepen to no more than 15 feet. Tightlining with minnows (Kentucky Lake rig) is unbeatable for fall crappie on the dropoffs. Structure decides the location of crappie and a depth finder is a must for effective fishing.

Trolling is another proven fall method which is good in all types of lakes from lowlands to highlands. On highland and midland lakes, it is by far the most consistent producer. A similar presentation with the same types of lures used in the spring and summer is employed in the fall. Trolling territory is identical to that of late spring except the area is much reduced by the fall drawdown and the crappie are more concentrated in remaining cover.

On lowland lakes and rivers, trolling is tremendously successful throughout the fall months until the snow flies.

In the fall, crappie migrate into shoreline cover and remain there for several weeks.

Arkansas

"I'd just as soon fish in the fall as the spring," says Charlie Beavers of Harrison, Arkansas, who plies his trade on the big Ozark impoundments of Table Rock and Bull Shoals. "Both these highland lakes are on the White River and are physically alike in size, depth, water color, bluffs, rocky banks, underwater contours, and fall drawdown. Table Rock differs in that it has more standing timber. One's as good as the other and I'm not sure I can't catch more in the fall than in the spring. At the end of summer, crappie are lying on bluffs or in the middle of pockets 30 to 35 feet deep.

"As the water cools in September, fish rise up to a shallower ledge on bluffs and to the edges of the pockets, or on the inside points of coves. I have better luck in the fall by staying near the main body of the lake and in pockets just off the main body. Those pockets that have less contact with the sun cool off quicker in September and crappie shallow up sooner in them.

"Minnows are better early in the fall because of the depth and water clarity, although I often use a jig tipped with a minnow. Two other ways to use minnows is to fish them like a jig with a split shot 18 inches above a gold hook run through the eyes. Gentle casts are made into 12 to 18 feet of water and retrieved slowly. The second way is to hook a minnow through the tail for fishing straight down over brush in deeper water.

"Brush is the key to my success," continues Charlie. "I've put out 35 to 40 beds since last year—mostly cedar trees and sycamores anchored with concrete blocks. Make sure the bed stands straight up and down or the crappie won't use them as well. They won't use all of them anyway. And only a few fish will be around each bed if they like the location. I catch one or two fish off a bed, move to another and catch one there, three at another and so on. If you run out of beds, start over again.

"By October 1 in normal years, crappie should be in a 12- to 15-foot zone. On really cool mornings, they'll move up into three to six feet of water. At this point, I switch entirely to a "Puddle Jumper." It's a jig with a uniquely shaped plastic body. Crappie really get on these in Bull Shoals and Table Rock in late October and November. My favorite "Jumper" is a $1/16$-ounce black jighead with white eyes and a purplish-brown body. I don't know why they like that combination but I've experimented with all others and they just hit it better. During deer season, I'm out here all by myself having a ball with these fall Ozark crappie!"

The "Puddle Jumper", made by the Mar Lynn Lure Company, Box 296, Blue Springs, MO 64015 is also popular on Kentucky Lake where guide Malcolm Lane extols its virtues. A similar lure is made by Mister Twister who calls it a "Katydid."

Charlie Brewer's concept of weedless jigheads and soft plastic bodies is unexcelled for probing crappie cover.

According to Charlie, trolling a "Puddle Jumper" behind a Hellbender or Martin Lizard is a good method through the month of September up to the middle of October. Lantern fishing remains productive about as long as you can stand the cold—usually the end of October in the Ozarks. Minnows are preferred after dark by anglers on pontoon boats who anchor on bluffs, bridges and in the mouths of coves. Crappie usually hold in a band of water from 16 to 24 feet. Below them at 25 to 35 feet are the white bass and below the whites are rainbow trout!

Charlie says, "Crappie are still biting pretty good by the first of December and are reasonably shallow. Of course, it all depends on the weather. They'll stay in the same places but go deeper if it gets very cold. By the middle of December, crappie fishing is pretty well done."

Iowa

By the middle of December, Iowa's Lake Rathbun could be frozen over but there's some prime fall crappie fishing in Rathbun in September, October and November.

Rathbun is a Corps of Engineers' flood control and water conservation project which was completed in 1969 on the Chariton River in South Central Iowa. The 11,000 acre impoundment has 155 miles of shoreline in rolling hill country that is intensely farmed. It muddies up quickly because of the farmland and the clay soil tends to "suspend" and it takes a little longer to clear up in the spring but in the fall there's rarely a problem with dingy water. Highway 142 crosses the South Fork of the Chariton and the main channel of the Chariton near the upper one-third of the reservoir. Upstream of these bridges, timber was left standing for fish and wildlife values. Much of the timber has rotted and broken off at the waterline which makes for tricky navigation but excellent crappie fishing. These timbered areas are exceptional in the spring and, to a lesser degree, in the fall for both black crappie and white crappie.

Jim Bruce, Iowa fishery biologist, recommends drifting with the wind across deep water with beetle spins searching for suspended schools of crappie. The jig-and-minnow combination is also good for drift fishing in the fall. Put out four or five jigs rigged at different depths with various colors of beetle spins and plain beetles without the spinner.

Glen Fowler of Melrose, Iowa, fishes Rathbun year round for crappie, even during the winter through the ice. Glen says, "Rathbun is one of the cleanest lakes in Iowa and has some fabulous crappie fishing. I've fished all over the country and it just doesn't get any better than what I've got right here at home. In the fall, schools of crappie begin to move from summer haunts along the Chariton river channel into shallower water around brush, rocks, timber, roadbeds, and dikes. There're some isolated areas where original brush is still present but it's like looking for a needle in a haystack. We're beginning to add our own cedar trees to supplement the loss of natural cover."

Minnows and jigs are used to catch Iowa crappie but Glen prefers live minnows. He fishes an eight-foot spinning rod and four- to six-pound Stren line. When he locates a structure on his depth finder, he hooks a minnow one of three ways: behind the dorsal fin, which makes the minnow swim away from the hook; through the eyes; or when using a floating jig, down through the nose. Glen says, "Fish holding structure is not hard to find in this lake and there'll always be some fish on it because Rathbun's full of crappie!"

In addition to still fishing over structures, Glen also trolls in the flat. His technique is rather unique in that he uses planeing boards which he runs out on either side of the boat about 25 yards. Although designed for walleye fishing, Glen takes a lot of Iowa crappie on this rig! "Anybody can make 'em," says Glen. "Take a small board with a piece of aluminum on the front. Bevel one board one way and the other the other way so they'll run true. A line is attached to the board for trolling shad-colored 1/4-ounce Shap Raps or Model A Bombers. When a fish hits, the line comes off the board and the fight is on."

One of Glen's favorite trolling passes is across an old dike built by a farmer before the lake was impounded to keep the Chariton river from flooding his crops. Crappie tend to lay along either side of the underwater dike.

Texas

In east Texas, near Edgewood, specifically lakes Tawakoni, Cedar Creek and Fork, trolling is rarely used as a method to catch crappie. "Nobody trolls on these lakes," says Jimmy Orsborn, who along with Bill Smith of Edgewood, Texas, won the 1988 crappiethon tournament on Cedar Creek. "Just about everybody either casts jigs or vertical fishes with jigs or minnows. There's a locally popular jigging rod which is a 6 1/2- to 7-foot spinning rod blank with a fly reel. It's ideal for probing into tiny holes in heavy brush or vertical fishing in stumpfields and standing timber along creek channel dropoffs."

These three Texas reservoirs are all top-notch crappie producers, two of which (Tawakoni and Cedar Creek) share similar characteristics of size, topography, water color, and forage species. Tawakoni's 33,000 acres are spread thin over an average depth of 15 feet and winter drawdown is about four feet. The lake has a great deal of standing timber and moss beds are beginning to reappear after a two-year absence.

Cedar Creek is only slightly smaller than Tawakoni and has roughly the same amount of standing timber (30%). Cedar Creek is named after one of its tributaries to the Trinity River and was completed in 1975.

Lake Fork is five years younger than Cedar Creek and dams up Fork Creek, a tributary to the Sabine River. Fork's 27,000 acres are clearer than either Tawakoni or Cedar Creek, which has resulted in more aquatic vegetation and a predominantly black crappie population. Almost half of the reservoir has standing timber and it is less susceptible to winds than the other two.

If big lakes aren't your bag, there are 25 smaller lakes ranging in size from 1,000 to 6,000 acres within a 60-mile radius of Edgewood which is on Highway

80 just east of Dallas. Most, if not all of these lakes, have outstanding crappie fishing. There're literally too many places to fish! This just might be the crappie center of the U.S.!

"Timing is critical in fall fishing on Texas lakes," says Jimmy Orsborn. "Crappie movements are dependent on rainfall and cold fronts. A good rain will raise the lake in September and send crappie into the creeks where they'll stay until spring, at least those with deep holes. In September and October, anglers tightline the creek channel dropoffs with jigs or minnows or probe into brush, stumps, and standing timber with a long pole and a black and yellow jig. We tie our own marabou jigs on a #six jig hook and a $1/16$-ounce head, usually in two colors. Black and yellow is a favorite combination on Tawakoni followed by blue/white and red/white.

"By or during November, depending on the weather, crappie move into the deeper holes of the creek for the winter. At this time, I leave my boat at home and walk the banks of the creek with a 16-foot pole and jig. With a pole of this length, I can reach the middle of the creek, fish the jig deep and start it up the side. I catch a lot of crappie in late fall with that method."

Two other patterns also work in the fall in addition to the creeks: bridges and marinas. Bridges are a prime summer hangout and crappie are reluctant to leave them in the fall because of the shade, cover, current, and minnows—all of the necessities of life. Orsborn says to work the columns and crossbeams with $1/16$-ounce jigs. Crappie often lay under the crossbeams where the undertow of the lake pulls a jig under the beam and into a crappie hang-out. Line-watching is imperative as the jig is controlled by the current and there's less ability to "feel" the strike.

Line-watching is also important in the marina pattern although there's no current involved. Fish are suspended at different depths (10 feet is a good norm) and counting down a jig to the holding zone while concentrating on the line is productive. When the water first starts cooling off, crappie begin to migrate from the main lake into the protected deep water coves occupied by marinas. Tawakoni has from 15 to 20 marinas on her 30,000 acres.

Many of the marina's slip owners sink brush into their boat well deep enough so the tops won't scratch a boat hull. It then becomes a matter of fishing down a row of boatstalls until you find the ones lined with brush. Please don't insist on fishing in a space being fished by the slip owner and his guests. Find your own; there'll be a number of others.

"In winter or late fall, marinas are the hottest pattern on the lake," says Orsborn. "I've broken ice a number of times going into a marina and caught fish every time!"

Missouri

At this point in the book, you may begin to think that you've got a pretty good handle on crappie behavior and the characteristics of different types of reservoirs. I hope so anyway. But before you become too complacent, let me introduce a lake that is antithetical to most others in the summer and fall—Harry S. Truman lake on the Osage River near Warsaw, Missouri.

Truman was completed in 1979 as a hydropower and flood control reservoir with a surface area of 55,600 acres at normal pool (second largest in Missouri). The 126-foot dam sits in the headwaters of the slightly larger and more famous Lake of the Ozarks. Above the dam, the water depth is only about 70 feet and it shallows up to 40 feet in the river and tributary channels farther upstream before giving way to a 20-foot average depth in the upper end. Numerous flats with five to seven feet of water are scattered throughout the reservoir as well as 8,800 acres of standing timber.

The 958 miles of shoreline encompass almost two different types of lake—the lower end is clear and lies in the Ozark highlands while the upper end is dingy and lies in flatland prairie topography. This factor is different in itself but two other factors separate this fishing and hunting paradise from the rest: the multipurpose pool gets lower in the summer than any other time of year and RISES in the fall! Crappie are caught all summer in water less than 10 feet deep!

A programmed fall rise is a most unusual water manipulation for the Corps of Engineers. But God bless 'em for this benevolent practice—it not only creates a longer fall crappie season, it provides a veritable haven for migrating waterfowl and makes for an ideal fall combination trip. Contact Lance Sullentrop at Sterett Creek Marina, Rt. 4, Box 354; Warsaw, Missouri 65355 (816) 438-2280 for more information.

In the summer, a shallow thermocline which runs from 7- to 10-feet deep keeps crappie concentrated in the more oxygenated surface layers of the lake. "Crappie are easy to locate in the summer," says Rich Abdollar, a Corps' Park Ranger on Truman. "They'll usually school around trees, bridges, off points, and along old channels sitting on the thermocline. If you find the right tree, a quick limit is assured. I use a long pole to flip Charlie Brewer's crappie grubs around standing timber. In the upper end where the water has more color to it, chartreuse and chartreuse/glitter is a favorite while on the lower end, white is a good choice.

"Bridge piers are also good," continues Rick. "Flipping a jig around them works in the daytime, while at night, fishing minnows under the lights is effective. Another prime night fishing location is the mouth of a major tributary. Shad cruise the open water of the main lake during the day but move into the tributaries at night. A boat anchored in the channel or on either side of the channel is in position to intercept this movement of crappie as they follow the shad."

Sometimes in early September, the first cool, wet-weather spell moves across Missouri and starts cooling off the tributaries. Shad, sensitive to even these slight temperature changes, start migrating into the tributaries followed by the crappie. Fall rains initiate an even stronger movement upstream.

Normal fall rises are two to six feet—the higher the rise, the farther the migration extends up the tributary. Strangely, the crappie, according to Rich

Abdollar, do not venture into the flooded flats but prefer to stay on trees and secondary points near the creek channel. Another curious thing happens; as the water cools, the thermocline deepens and the crappie get deeper!

The summer/fall pattern is in reverse on Truman—crappie are shallow in the summer and go deeper in the Fall.

Nighttime fishing is still good through September. By late October, crappie start moving back to winter quarters. Tightlining with a single rod and a heavy split shot or two hooks with a bell sinker on the end (Kentucky Lake Rig) becomes effective on crappie now on deep structure in 20 feet of water. Truman anglers change their preference from jigs to minnows for late fall fishing.

Southwest

In the arid desert country of the Southwest, fall fishing comes later in the season (November, December) but once it starts, it doesn't stop for winter. Crappie fishing gets even better in January and February and right into spring when it picks up still another notch!

So there is no winter lull on lakes such as Arizona's Roosevelt Reservoir and the nearby San Carlos impoundment on the San Carlos Indian Reservation near Globe.

Lewis Barry of Phoenix, who teamed with David Rosenbarger to win the 1988 Crappiethon tournament on Roosevelt says that Roosevelt is an outstanding crappie hole and San Carlos is even better. "It starts getting really good in November and stays that way until May.

"San Carlos is smaller," says Lewis. "But it's not as old as Roosevelt and consequently it has more brushy cover in the lake and produces bigger crappie. A license from the Indian Reservation is required to fish in the clear waters of San Carlos. Occasionally the lake muddies up from rains and the crappie move down in front of the advancing dingy water."

Both reservoirs are plateau types which tend to be long and straight with little arms that don't run very far back into the hills. Like midland lakes, they can be roughly divided into thirds to forecast crappie movements. The upper third, with its shallow flats are sought out in the spring, the middle third holds fish in the fall and the lower third near the dam holds fish in the fall, and also holds "suspended" schools of crappie throughout the summer. Roosevelt differs with this scheme because it has two major rivers (Tonto & the Salt) which come together from opposite directions.

Lewis Barry, armed with an 11-foot, 6-inch graphite pole, a cheap reel and 6-pound test line, depends on his 4-ID to locate schools of fish on rock shelves in coves off the main lake body. Only one pole per fisherman is allowed in Arizona for crappie fishing. Spider rigs and multi-pole trolling outfits are illegal! You can't catch 'em as fast but you can catch 'em all day because there's no creel limit!

Once the school is located, Lewis drops a white or chartreuse mini-jig in either $1/16$- or $1/8$-ounce into the gathering. Occasionally he opts for a $1/4$-ounce size if the fish are deeper.

The Southwest's more celebrated canyon lakes, Havasau on the California border, Mohave and Mead forming the southwest tip of Nevada, and mammoth size Lake Powell on the Utah border, have all been infested with striped bass gangs which have practically wiped out the local crappie populations. But there's some super striper fishing—probably the best in the country. For stripers, contact Bob Gripentog, Las Vegas Marina; Lake Mead; Box 771; Henderson, Nevada 89015; 702-565-9111.

For great fall crappie fishing that skips winter, head for Arizona's Roosevelt and San Carlos reservoirs.

Keep in mind that the fall migration may occur earlier than you thought it could and it will probably last longer than you thought it would. Once crappie are in their fall pattern, they tend to stay with it for weeks on end. It's the most consistent and pleasant fishing of the year......and the loneliest!

Best Crappie Lakes

Chapter XVIII

Naming the "best" of anything is a dangerous pastime that adds enemies and often accounts for the loss of friends.

With that thought in mind, let me make it perfectly clear that the following list of "Best Crappie Lakes" is by no means inclusive and I can think of at least twice as many other lakes that should be included but space won't permit.

Kentucky Lake - Barkley Lake

Although these two lakes are on different river systems, I mention both of them together because they are joined by a canal and can be fished in the same day. An angler can camp in TVA's Land Between the Lakes and fish one lake in the morning and the other in the afternoon! Despite their geographic similarity, each impoundment has its own personality and requires separate study to solve the whereabouts of crappie.

Kentucky Lake

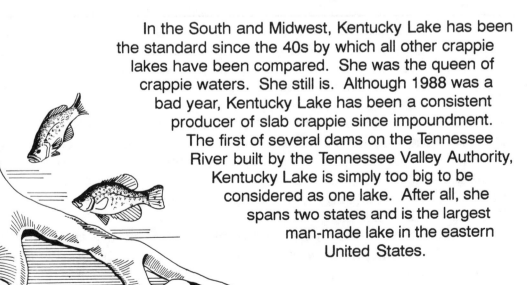

In the South and Midwest, Kentucky Lake has been the standard since the 40s by which all other crappie lakes have been compared. She was the queen of crappie waters. She still is. Although 1988 was a bad year, Kentucky Lake has been a consistent producer of slab crappie since impoundment. The first of several dams on the Tennessee River built by the Tennessee Valley Authority, Kentucky Lake is simply too big to be considered as one lake. After all, she spans two states and is the largest man-made lake in the eastern United States.

Her 160,300 acres stretch a shoreline of 2,400 mile and so it becomes necessary to break the monolith into small pieces. Crappie fishermen usually have their favorite Kentucky Lake fishing grounds broken down into one tributary or one bay. A band of devotees may spend their annual spring vacation on Jonathan Creek, Blood River, Ginger Bay, Redd Hollow, Big Sandy River, Cuba Landing, Perryville, Birdsong Creek, etc.

Because of her size, convenient interstate access is available from practically any direction and once you arrive, there are ample facilities and services at all access points.

Kentucky Lake is a typical lowland impoundment with a five foot difference in winter and summer pool. The drop to winter pool (354.0 feet) begins in July and reaches it by November. The rise to summer pool (359.0 feet) begins in April in normal years without an influx of flood waters. The spring rise puts water into a perimeter of shoreline buttonball bushes where spawning takes place and most of the crappie are caught.

After spawning, fishing consists of casting jigs to planted brushpiles (there's no standing timber) or probing channel dropoffs with a tightline rig. Trolling is popular throughout the summer and into the fall. Winter fishing is excellent on the deeper channel dropoffs.

Guides and resorts are too numerous to list separately; for information contact: Kentucky Lake Vacationland, Rt. 7 Box 145, Gilbertsville, KY 42044, (502) 362-8124; Lakeland Guide Service, Rt. 2 Box 327, Gilbertsville, KY 42044, (502) 362-8124. In the Tennessee portion, contact; Paris-Henry County Chamber of Commerce, 104 Caldwell, Paris, TN 38242, (901) 642-3431; Guide Steve McCadams, Rt. 1 Box 432, Springville, TN 38256, (901) 642-0360.

Barkley

Barkley came along 20 years after Kentucky Lake and she has constantly labored to match the quality of her neighbor's crappie fishing. In the last few years, that goal has been reached and Barkley has really come into her own.

Impounded by the Corps of Engineers in 1966 on the Cumberland River less than two miles from the paralleling Tennessee River, the Corps and the TVA elected to build a canal to connect the two river systems.

Barkley differs from her neighbor by being several degrees cooler, smaller (18 miles long, 57,000 acres) and has more sharply defined creek and river channels because of her relatively younger age. Because she is younger, her shoreline hasn't been washed clean of soil and clay as has been the case on Kentucky. The result is a reservoir that is dingier and allows a closer approach to shallow water crappie.

Fishing techniques consist of casting jigs in February and March to schools located on dropoffs; minnow fishing in the bushes and brushpiles in April; trolling in early and late summer, and back to jigs in the fall.

Because there's no standing timber in the lake, fish relate to stumps and brush on meandering creek channels throughout the length of the lowland

Lake Barkley Under Construction

At the top of the picture is Kentucky Lake. The two impoundments were joined by a canal at the narrowest point of the Tennessee and Cumberland River systems near Grand Rivers, Kentucky.

impoundment. The scarcity of natural cover has prompted numerous introductions of man-made fish attractors by individuals and state agencies. Attractors are the real key to successful crappie fishing on Lake Barkley.

Services and facilities are excellent—there are public campgrounds (fee required), launching ramps, resorts, marinas, and bait shops. Contact: Buzzard Rock Resort, Box 191, Kuttawa, KY 42055, (502) 388-2532; Prizer Point Marina, Rt. 4 Box 219, Cadiz, KY 42211, (502) 522-3762; Bumpas Mills Marina, Rt. 1 Box 46A, Bumpas Mills, TN 37028, (610) 232-5238; Kuttawa Harbor, Kuttawa, KY 42055, (502) 388-9563; Eddy Creek Marina, Rt. 1, Eddyville, KY 42038, (502) 388-7743.

Weiss

Weiss Lake is located in northeast Alabama a few miles east of Interstate 59 between Gadsen and Ft. Payne. Construction of the 30,200 acre reservoir on the Coosa River was completed in 1961 by the Alabama Power Company.

Almost immediately, stringers of slab crappie began coming out of the submerged ditches, creeks and sloughs that once separated bottomland cornfields. Limits of 50 fish a day became and remain common.

The crappie fishery has been maintained the past two decades by an abundant shad crop and the excellent water quality of the lake's three major tributaries: the Coosa is by far the largest but the Chattooga River and Little River add considerable inflow.

Originating in nearby Georgia, the Coosa has most of the lake's standing timber and numerous shallow flats and is the first of the trio to entertain spring time visitors. Because the Coosa warms up faster, you'll find crappie less than 10 feet deep while those in Little River are still in deep winter holding areas. Somewhere in between these two is the Chattooga with its own pattern. The result is a longer spring season enjoyed by fishermen who switch from one to the other as temperatures change.

J.R. Tucker, owner of J.R.'s Marina on Weiss Lake, likes to use light spinning tackle to cast jigs or a cork and jig combination around boat docks, piers and boathouses in the springtime.

Water clarity is another bonus of the three rivers—rarely will they all be muddy at the same time. The Coosa's water tends to get dirty quicker and stay muddy longer while Little River rarely gets dingy.

Wading is an excellent method on Weiss to catch spawning crappie in the backs of coves and pockets. Casting jigs or a cork and jig is productive around piers, stumps, and brushpiles. When they first return to deep water, guide Joe Rattray switches to ultralight spinning gear and $1/_{16}$- and $1/_{32}$-ounce chartreuse or motor oil twister tail grubs. His favorite type of structure is a hump or high spot loaded with stumps next to a channel dropoff.

As October and November roll in, the crappie fishing picks up again in shallow water by casting jigs around cover and structure in 6 to 12 feet of water.

For information, contact: Joe Rattray, Riverside Campground, Cedar Bluff, AL 35959, (205) 779-6117; J.R.'s Marina, Cedar Bluff, AL 35959, (205) 779-6461; Guide Tim Horton, (205) 779-6680.

Mississippi River

Perhaps it's not fair to mention the Mississippi River as one of the best crappie areas because of its length and the myriad numbers of oxbows, sloughs, creeks and rivers that are part of it. But, it wouldn't be fair to single out any one section as being better than the rest because it's too hard to do. "Ole Miss" is simply a top-notch crappie producer from Minnesota to Louisiana.

In the upper Mississippi Valley above St. Louis, 27 locks and dams maintain a nine-foot navigation depth for barges. The tailwaters of these dams provide a year-round crappie fishery during normal flows. When the Big Muddy gets rowdy in the spring, it's time to follow her out into the backwaters.

During the summer when she's low, crappie tend to stay near the main channel in deep holes or in the deeper sloughs off the river when there is some current. Bob Monaghan of Camanche, Iowa, often has good luck fishing the wooden pilings around grain terminals or in sand and gravel quarries connected to the main stream. Bob says that each dam has its own level which dictates the location of crappie. At Lock and Dam 12 and 13 near Clinton, Iowa, the best all around depth is 10 feet. If it gets higher, 12 to 13 feet, water gets into the bottoms and disperses the fish over a wide area.

Launching ramps are plentiful along the Upper Mississippi; guides are harder to find. In the Clinton area, contact: Bob Monaghan, 1519 Third St., Camanche, IA 52732, (319) 259-8909 or Bill's Bait Shop, 2014 N. Second St., Clinton, IA 52732, (319) 243-4696.

In the lower Mississippi Valley below St. Louis, there aren't any locks and dams to stem the flow of the big river and I hope there never will be.

Because of the force of the flow, the navigation hazards (floating logs, sandbars, dikes, buoys) and the amount of barge traffic, the Mississippi is a dangerous place to boat. Stay off it if at all possible and trailer around to a secluded cutoff or oxbow to fish. That's where the crappie will be anyway. Springtime fishing usually means following the spring rise into the bottoms. In the summer when the river's low, crappie "suspend" in the deepest part of the old oxbows where trolling is in wide practice.

Trolling is still productive in the fall but many fish move into the edge of dead timber or live willows for several weeks, and are taken on cane poles and minnows or a fly rod and tube jig.

The main difference in crappie fishing between the Upper and Lower Mississippi River Valley is that you don't fish the main channel in the lower regions and you do in the upper.

Numerous fishing camps are scattered along both sides of the Mississippi and the operators will point you in the right direction because guides usually aren't available. Rent a boat, cut a willow for a pole, buy some minnows and you're in business!

Excellent maps of the Mississippi River are available at Corps of Engineer District offices in Rock Island, St. Louis, Memphis, Vicksburg and New Orleans.

Reed Bullard of Memphis, Tennessee snakes a crappie out of the willows at Tunica Cutoff, an old oxbow of the Mississippi River. Water levels were dropping on the outside edge of the willowline and open water.

D'Arbonne

D'Arbonne is the home of the Golden crappie I mentioned in Chapter One. To my knowledge, it is the only body of water to have produced such an unusual coloration.

Located just north of Interstate 20 a few miles northwest of Monroe, Louisiana, this 15,000 acre impoundment is a dandy crappie spot.

Formed by the construction of a dam and spillway across Bayou D'Arbonne 10 miles southeast of Farmerville in 1963, the average depth is 8.5 feet and the shoreline is 150 miles long.

A total of 5,200 acres of timber have been cleared which allows better fisherman access to its more remote corners. Of this cleared area, over 900 acres are located in front of the spillway with the balance scattered along the banks of Bayou D'Arbonne and Corney Bayou. The remainder of the lake is flooded oak, tupelo gum, and cypress.

Aquatic vegetation has taken a good hold in the form of coontail moss, hydrilla and lily pads but it doesn't prohibit catching crappie. Dr. Bill Miller, III of Monroe, Louisiana, loves to fish the grass by quietly slipping along the outside edges of a weedline and dropping a minnow or jig into shady pockets.

In the open water areas, trolling is popular and there are three bridges which attract and hold crappie in summer and winter.

Other productive areas include: the creek channels where enterprising fishermen have sunk brushpiles along the dropoffs; pilings and brushpiles put in by the Louisiana Bass Federation at numerous locations.

In the winter, "yo-yo" fishing is practiced by those who don't like to stop fishing on account of cold weather. The method is in wide usage throughout the lower Mississippi River Valley wherever there's standing timber in the water. A Yo-Yo is a spring loaded device with a hook and short line wound into a metal holder about the size of a real yo-yo. It's tied to a tree or limb and baited with a minnow about two feet deep. Depending on your supply and seriousness, you should set out between 15 and 50! Even during the coldest days, enough crappie will be swimming in the timber to make yo-yoing worthwhile.

When the fish hits the minnow, the yo-yo is triggered and reels him up to the top until the fisherman comes along and takes him off. And don't get caught running someone else's yo-yos! There's not a great deal of sport to it but it's still a lot of fun.

Cabins and camping facilities are available at D'Arbonne; guides may be harder to find. Contact the Louisiana Department of Wildlife and Fisheries, 400 Royal St., New Orleans, LA 70130, (504) 568-5612 for more information on D'Arbonne.

Truman

Truman's as great a lake as her namesake—"The buck stops here" Harry S. Truman. Located about 40 miles northeast of Truman's birthplace in Lamar, Missouri, and only 1 ½ miles from Warsaw, the dam was completed in 1979.

The 126-foot high, concrete and earth embankment backs up the Osage River to include over 55,600 acres of normal pool, making it the largest flood control lake in Missouri. There are no navigation locks but six turbine generators are in place to produce electrical power. This means that when the generators are running, the pull of the current will draw crappie out of shallow water.

Nestled in rugged hills and hardwood forests on the Prairie-Ozark border, the scenic reservoir has an ideal combination of open water, points, bridges, riprap, channel dropoffs, and standing timber to please the most discriminating crappie fisherman.

Add a bonus of turkey hunting in the spring, deer and small game hunting in the fall, and waterfowl in the winter and you have the makings of paradise! The Corps of Engineers purchased 100,000 acres of land around the lake which is open to public hunting with the exception of developments such as campgrounds, picnic areas, beaches, and marinas.

Don't forget to stop by the Corps' resource management office to pick up a free Golden Age Passport for people over 62, which entitles the holder to a 50% discount on camping at all Corps facilities. A Golden Access Passport is also available to the blind and disabled.

Nearly 9,000 acres of standing timber were left in the lake for crappie fishing. I guess the crappie let some other species use it for special occasions! The timber is probably the best direction a crappie fisherman could take for consistent success. Concentrate on points of land in the timber and along old channels.

Truman is the recipient of three major rivers (Pomme de Terre, Osage and the South Grand), four if you include the Sac River which merges with the Osage near Osceola, and numerous creeks. All of these arteries are crossed by bridges which are excellent spots for land based fishermen as well as boaters.

For info, contact; Resource Manager Truman Lake, Rt. 2 Box 29A, Warsaw, MO 65355, (815) 438-2280, Manager Jim Murphy; Bucksaw Point Marina, Rt. 3 Box 181, Clinton, MO 64735, (800) 331-4072; Osage Bluff Marina, HCR 67, Box 86C, Warsaw, MO 65355, (816) 438-2934.

Palestine

Palestine is a 27,000 acre impoundment of the Neches River just southwest of Tyler, Texas. The "Y"-shaped lake lies north/south between rolling hills and flatland covered with pines and grasslands. The lack of agriculture in the drainage basin helps keep the lake's waters clear to semi-stained throughout the year......unlike her neighbor 40 miles due west—Cedar Creek Lake.

The Neches River Authority completed Palestine over 20 years ago, but about 12 years ago, they nearly doubled the original size of the lake by raising the level another 20 feet......a level that remains very stable all year. Springtime rises are rarely three feet above normal and the summer pool is about the same.

Hundreds of acres of standing timber are located in the upper end of both of the major arms of the lake—productive areas for spawning crappie. Aquatic vegetation is not prevalent but it is beginning to make more of an appearance. In the lower end, there are a number of piers and boathouses owned by shore-line residents which offer crappie structure in the spring, summer, and fall.

In early spring, the water's so clear that casting jigs is preferred over minnows unless the water does get a little dingier. After the spawn may be a more productive time on this east Texas lake. It definitely is for Guide Al Matura who does most of his serious fishing in May, June, and into July until the water temperature hits 90°! Al says, "When the surface temp is 90, I lose 'em and I quit guiding."

Prior to that, however, Al racks up limits for his clients deep-water-structure fishing with the latest in electronic gear. Al's Ranger 375 is outfitted with four depth machines—a flasher and papergraph on the console and a LCR and a flasher on the bow. With these underwater eyes he can probe submerged trees along feeder creeks and the main channel with jigs and minnows. Palestine is not a deep lake and crappie are usually located in the bottom 10 feet of 20-foot water.

One of the best times for Palestine crappie is the dead of winter—mid-January—when the crappie congregate along the old river channel just above the dam in water 35 to 60 feet deep! A regular convention of boats (sometimes over 300!) gathers for this deep freeze action.

Al recommends small jigs ($1/16$- or $1/8$-ounce) and feels there's no way you can go wrong with white! Contact: Al Matura, Rt. 1 Box 1636, Chandler, TX 75758, (214) 849-3489.

Carlyle Lake

Carlyle Lake is located on the Kaskaskia River 107 miles above its confluence with the mighty Mississippi and 50 miles due east of St. Louis near the town of Carlyle, Illinois.

Completed in June of 1967, the 67-foot high dam (above the stream bed) backs up 26,000 acres of water at summer pool (Elev. 445.0) with a shoreline of 83 miles. The lake is rectangularly shaped, two to three miles wide, 15 miles long, and lies roughly north/south. Maximum depth is 35 feet and the overall average depth is 11 feet. These numbers should tell you that Carlyle is a shallow, flatland type of reservoir which does not have deep inlets and is thus very hard to fish on windy days. Don't take refuge in the standing timber in the upper third of the reservoir during a high wind—flooded timber has a nasty habit of breaking in the tops and becoming a lethal pile driver.

The timber is where you want to be in the spring, however, when both black crappie and white crappie move into the shallow depths to spawn. Like crappie everywhere, they use migration routes to get to the spawning territory. A major movement occurs along the old Kaskaskia River channel to intersections with ditches, sloughs and creeks such as Bear, Hurricane, Maggot, East Fork and West Fork, each of which tap off a portion of the migrating crappie.

Two public access areas, Tamilco on the west and Patoka on the east, provide launching ramps to serve the upper end. Patoka also offers overnight camping.

Just downstream where the timber ends at the Burlington Northern Railroad, two marinas, Keyesport on the west, (618) 749-5121, and Boulder on the east bank, (618) 226-3223, provide services and facilities for crappie fishermen.

From this point, the lower two-thirds of the lake is open water with the exception of standing timber left in three of the major bays. Two Illinois Department of conservation state parks, three Corps of Engineer recreation areas and the Dam West Marina, (618) 594-2461, serve fishermen on the lower end.

Summer time fishing can be productive if you can locate a concentration of fish in deeper water—but not over 12 feet deep. From mid-June to September, the dissolved oxygen content becomes too low below 12 feet. Tightlining with minnows is the preferred method and local experts add a small, white beetle body on the hook with the minnow.

Mid-September to mid-November is harvest time as crappie come back to shallow water and fatten up for the winter. After November, there is occasionally some good ice fishing where there is solid ice cover of six inches or more. Ice fishing is practiced with small minnows and insect larvae (mousies, waxworm, goldenrod grub, corn borer) in combination with an artificial ice fly. For more information, contact: Carlyle Lake Mgmt. Office, R.R. 1, Carlyle, IL 62231-9703, (618) 594-2484, and IL Dept of Conser., R.R. 3, Carlyle, IL 62231, (618) 594-3015.

Tenn/Tom Waterway

The Tennessee-Tombigbee Waterway which connects the Tennessee River with the Gulf of Mexico was the most environmentally scrutinized water project in our nation's history. As a result, fishery biologists were able to make and implement recommendations to benefit the fishery resource prior to construction.

The 234 miles of waterway are stair stepped with ten locks and dams before it joins the Black Warrior River near Demopolis, Alabama. It represents a "chain of lakes" whose collective 44,000 acres are full of crappie.

Beginning at its northern end, the Tenn/Tom runs south from Pickwick Lake's Yellow Creek to Bay Springs Lake near Tupelo, Mississippi. This 6,700

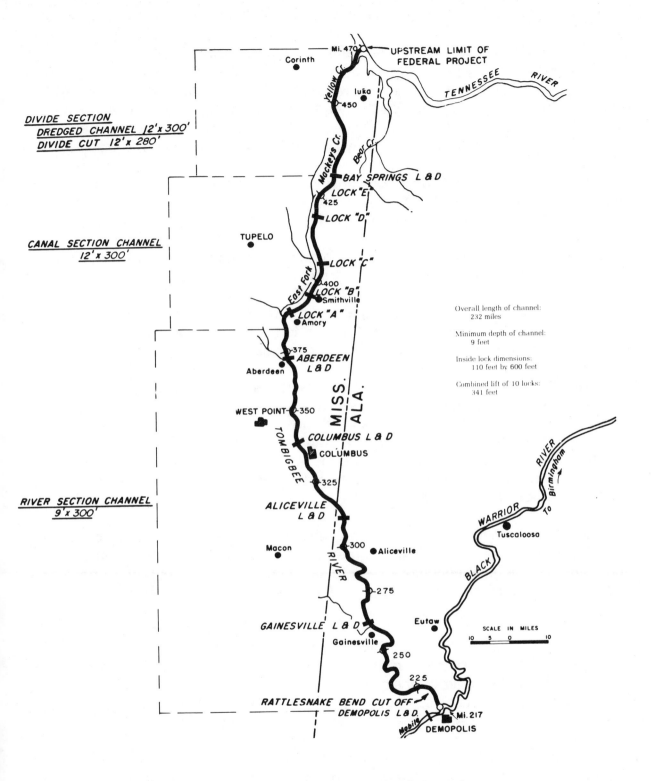

DIVIDE SECTION
DREDGED CHANNEL 12'x 300'
DIVIDE CUT 12'x 280'

CANAL SECTION CHANNEL
12'x 300'

RIVER SECTION CHANNEL
9'x 300'

Corinth

Mi. 470 — UPSTREAM LIMIT OF
FEDERAL PROJECT

Iuka

TENNESSEE RIVER

450

Yellow Cr.

Bear Cr.

Mackeys Cr.

BAY SPRINGS L & D
LOCK "E"
425
LOCK "D"

TUPELO

LOCK "C"

East Fork

400
LOCK "B"
Smithville
LOCK "A"
Amory

375
ABERDEEN
L & D
Aberdeen

WEST POINT
350

Tombigbee

COLUMBUS L & D
COLUMBUS

325

MISS. ALA.

ALICEVILLE
L & D

Macon

300   Aliceville

RIVER

275

GAINESVILLE L & D

Eutaw

Gainesville

250

225

RATTLESNAKE BEND CUT OFF
DEMOPOLIS L & D.

Mobile

Mi. 217
DEMOPOLIS

Overall length of channel:
232 miles

Minimum depth of channel:
9 feet

Inside lock dimensions:
110 feet by 600 feet

Combined lift of 10 locks:
341 feet

WARRIOR   RIVER

To Birmingham

Tuscaloosa

BLACK

SCALE IN MILES
10   5   0   10

TENNESSEE - TOMBIGBEE WATERWAY

MISSISSIPPI AND ALABAMA

acre lake is deep and clear and has many coves and pockets filled with standing timber.

During the spring spawn from late March through April, fish tend to congregate in the timber as far back as they can go. After the spawn, they relate to deeper trees and brush near creek channel ledges or dropoffs. High spots are also worth prospecting for because they'll be covered with stumps and crappie, if they're not too deep.

Summertime fishing is most popular under the lights after dark because of the water clarity. Bay Springs is the clearest of the ten lakes and is more characteristic of highland reservoirs while the nine downstream are typically lowland by nature.

Below Bay Springs, the Canal Section has five locks simply labeled A, B, C, D, and E which have a water surface area of 6,100 acres. Although small in comparison to the river section, the locks provide perfect habitat for crappie. Each was created by constructing a levee on the west side of the canal's route and allowing the canal waters to flow naturally to high ground on the east side. The overflow inundates acre after acre of Tombigbee river bottomland and is a favorite area in spring and fall.

The River Section begins below Lock A with Aberdeen Lake's 4,100 acres, followed by Columbus (8,900 acres), Aliceville (8,300 acres), and Gainesville (6,400 acres). All four are fished essentially the same. In early spring, head for the pockets of timber, stopping first at the outer edges to check the deeper cover before making your way back through the maze of brush and trees. This is an area ideally suited for the venerable jon boat because when the crappie really get serious about spawning, they may be in water barely covering their dorsal fin!

Leave the casting gear at home and carry a long pole (10-14 feet) and some Slater jigs ($1/16$- or $1/8$-ounce) in green and orange, and a sculling paddle.

After spawning, crappie move back to flats near a dropoff that have cover and six to ten feet of water overhead. Aquatic weed patches will also harbor fish.

In the summer, they move from the flats to dropoffs on the main river channel or major tributaries which have a continual flow. Tightlining with minnows along these dropoffs is productive until the first cold front in September when they start on their fall migration.

Perhaps the most consistent year-round fishing is in the tailraces of the dams where at least a few crappie can always be caught by casting white, yellow, and chartreuse jigs.

Services and facilities are minimal on the waterway but they are being developed. Stock up at the nearest bait shop before getting to the lake. Columbus, Mississippi is the largest population center and is centrally located within a few miles of the Tenn/Tom. Contact Woods 'n Waters, 1920 Highway 45 North, Columbus, MS 39701, (610) 327-6814, for an up-to-date fishing report.

Reelfoot

Located in the extreme northwest corner of Tennessee, Reelfoot Lake is one of the most unique bodies of water in America. Her cypress studded, lily-pad choked acres are foreboding and mysterious in true swamp fashion and she resists intruders with millions of stumps beneath her surface—a result of a series of earthquakes in 1811/12 when giant bottomland hardwoods sank into the ground and the nearby Mississippi River flowed backwards for two days to fill the hole created by the quakes.

Reelfoot is approximately five miles wide, 14 miles long and consists of four main basins which are interconnected by natural sloughs or man-made canals although most lake visitors put in as close as possible to their chosen fishing area in order to keep boat runs to a minimum. You don't have to run far to be in productive territory and the aforementioned stumps will make you glad you don't.

A special "Reelfoot boat" (see Chapter on Boats) has been developed for use on the Earthquake Lake and is available for rent at the state park. A number of resorts are located along Highway 22 on the southern shore near Samburg for visiting sportsmen who have been coming to this aquatic wilderness since the 1800s.

Crappie fishing is excellent all year with the exception of unusually cold winters when the lake freezes over. Early spring finds crappie in the deepest water of the basins (12 to 14 feet) where anglers drift with several poles baited with minnows.

As the water warms, they move toward the shoreline to the outside edges of the deeper cypress trees before finally deploying into the shallows. Aquatic weeds are also used as spawning sites in the absence of woody cover. The aquatic weeds (lily pads, saw grass, bonnets, duckweed, etc.) have been an integral part of Reelfoot's colorful and often violent history. Their encroachment on open waters has reached alarming proportions and every method of control has been studied and many have been implemented, but the fight goes on.

In the summer, crappie return to deep water until September when they move into the stumps, trees, pads, and duckblinds in shallow water. There's very little opportunity to cast a jig on Reelfoot—the only way to fish is with a long pole and minnows or jigs. The water always has good "color" and a close approach can be made easily.

Despite the close proximity of productive cover to the resorts and fishing camps, it's a good idea to hire a guide to show you around. In the fall, Reelfoot offers an outstanding combination package of waterfowl hunting and crappie fishing. Or just plain bird watching. The lake is a birder's paradise. For information contact: Reelfoot Lake State Park, Rt. 1, Tiptonville, TN 38079, (901) 253-7756, and Arrowhead Lodge, Al and Vickie Hamilton, P.O. Box 223, Hornbeak, TN 38232, (901) 538-2371.

On Reelfoot Lake, nudge your cork and minnow as close as possible to the base of cypress trees and work completely around the tree before moving to the next.

Clarks Hill

Clarks Hill Lake has over 70,000 acres of the best fishing waters in the eastern United States and crappie ranks #1 in the numbers of fish caught. Approximately 30% of the lake still has standing timber and there are 1,200 miles of shoreline.

Located 22 miles upstream of Augusta, Georgia, Clarks Hill dam creates a midland type of reservoir on the Savannah River. The state lines of Georgia and South Carolina meet in the middle of the lake and run the entire length of the reservoir. A major tributary, Little River (there's also one on the South Carolina side) enters from the west just above the dam.

One of the largest Corps lakes in the Southeast, Clarks Hill takes advantage of its size and the absence of any really large metropolitan area nearby to offer quality fishing without a quantity of intruders. Many of which are devoting their efforts to other species such as stripers, hybrids, and largemouths.

Sonny Mason, who guides out of Clarks Hill Marina, says the best crappie fishing is usually found in the middle sections of the long impoundment from Buoy 48 to the Highway 378 bridge.

Spring action is typically in the flooded willows with a long pole and jigs or minnows. After spawning, crappie retreat to standing timber in 20 to 25 feet of water where live minnows are the better selection. Fish attractors planted by the Corps, Georgia's DNR and South Carolina's Wildlife and Marine Resources Department also provide concentration points.

Sonny says that very few crappie fishermen troll in the summer because of the stripers and hybrids who tend to have their way when hooked on a crappie outfit!

However, more than a few fish are caught under the lights at night during the summer. By the middle of September, crappie have moved up and into structure in 16 to 18 feet of water and will continue to migrate shallower until water temperatures become too cold. And then they make somewhat of an odd excursion to open water where they gather in huge schools suspended about 15 feet deep for the winter.

Winter drawdown is about 10 feet although droughts have kept summer water levels lower than normal. Stratification of the lake into three levels (Epilimnion, Thermocline, Hypolimnion) is a critical influencing factor in Clarks Hill Lake. Based on temperature differences, the thermocline is the key and crappie relate to it from late spring to early fall.

Clarks Hill has a wealth of facilities around her shores in numerous access points, marinas, campgrounds, resorts, and state parks. For more information, contact: Sonny Mason - Guide, P.O. Box 117, Plum Branch, SC 29845, (803) 443-5577; Dick Goodson - Guide, Clarks Hill Marina, P.O. Box 8A, Plum Branch, SC 29845, (803) 443-5577; and Resource Manager, Clarks Hill Lake, Clarks Hill, SC 29821, (803) 333-2476.

Buggs Island/John H. Kerr

As sometimes happens with Corps of Engineers projects, the popular local name for a dam is changed to honor a politician who helped make it a reality ......a practice I wish the Corps would abandon.

But whatever you call it, you can also call it a great crappie lake. Guide Jim Abers unabashedly calls Buggs Island the #1 crappie lake in Virginia and probably North Carolina, both of which happen to share this 48,900 acre body of water. Although the lion's share is in the commonwealth, each state honors the other's fishing license anywhere on the lake.

A 144-foot high dam was completed on the Roanoke River in 1953, just above Gaston, a lake developed by a private utility company. Eight hundred miles of deeply inletted shoreline fork into two main arms—Nutbush Creek in the North Carolina portion and the Roanoke River in Virginia which forks again near the headwaters of the lake.

Buggs Island is a midland type of impoundment which has no standing timber or beds of aquatic vegetation. Annual drawdown is no more than three or four feet. Where do the crappie stay? According to Jim Abers, they relate to either stumps, rocks, dropoffs, or manmade fish attractors. Jim prefers willow for his planted brushpiles because it's fairly forgiving when snagged. Sweet gum is also popular and is readily available. Check with the Corps' Resource Manager for a permit to put in fish attractors.

In early spring (March, April) look for the warmest cove you can find—water temperatures will range from the mid-40s to the mid-50s. Put out several 16- to 18-foot cane poles with one hook and minnow on each set at different depths. Crappie may be anywhere from two to 12 feet deep and will change depths during the course of the day. Drift across the cover with the wind if it's in the right direction or with the aid of a trolling motor if it's not. Jigs can be substituted for live minnows but Jim Abers prefers minnows for 90% of his crappie fishing on Buggs Island.

Late spring often finds lake levels flooding into the thick perimeter of willows and sweet gums where the fish are hard to get to. When they leave the heavy cover, the migration is back to dropoffs in the tributaries or to brushpiles.

In the summer, the dozen or so bridges spanning the lake attract anglers after dark where they fish under the lights. Those bridges nearest the main channel or on major creeks are best. Buggs Island has seven powerhouse turbines and their operation dictates the location of crappie in the summer as well as the spring and fall. When they're pulling a lot of water through the generators, crappie move out of shallow water to deeper water.

By mid-September, crappie start moving into a 15-foot range of water on the dropoffs but they are not extremely aggressive. A good fisherman probing the edge of a dropoff with a Kentucky Lake Rig and a depth finder can catch 25 to 30 fish a day. This ratio picks up significantly by October and lasts through mid-December; during which time catches of 50 to 100 become common and usually include a couple of citation fish. No, you won't be cited for catching over the limit (there's no size or creel limit in Virginia)—the state of Virginia issues a citation of achievement to an angler who catches a crappie weighing over two pounds! It's a nice award denoting the weight, date caught, the name of the fisherman, and is given on the spot by guides and marinas.

First timers to Buggs Island should definitely engage a guide for their initial day or trip in order to get a handle on the types of structures crappie are using at the time. But, as I've said before, don't go back to the guide's spots—find a similar set of circumstances. Here's who to contact at Buggs Island: Resource Manager, Corps of Engineers, Rt. 1, Box 76, Boydton, VA 23917, (804) 378-6662; Jim's Guide Service, P.O. Box 393, Boydton, VA 23917, (804) 372-3557; and Clarksville Marina, P.O. Box 747, Clarksville, VA 23927, (804) 374-8501.

Lake to Plate

Chapter XIX

We're finally getting down to the nitty-gritty, the real reason for going to all of the trouble and expense to catch a mess of scaly critters the wife may not let you bring in the kitchen. That is until she tastes a golden brown fillet of crappie. Ooooh! It is the food of gods. No cuisine can hold a candle to a platter of fried crappie! Why, she'll even begin to suggest that it's time for you to go crappie fishing again and will insist on cleaning the catch in the kitchen sink while you sit by the fire with an amoretto and coffee or by the pool with a Lynchburg Lemonade, depending on the season of course.

Despite the delicate nature of their flavor, crappie are a fairly resilient fish that will live through a lot of banging around in a livewell or on a fish stringer. If the water's cool enough (less than 75°) to keep them healthy, a livewell or a stringer is all right, although most of my stringers end up in the outboard prop before the day is over. If not, then they should be placed on ice and many fishermen do so regardless of season or water temperature. The only disadvantage of putting them on ice is that they don't take as pretty a picture! But that's more important to outdoor writers than most fishermen.

There are a couple of things that can be done to help keep crappie alive in the livewell. Obviously, an aerator is valuable but only if it functions properly. Keep it clean and turn it on regularly throughout the day. Ice added to livewells helps keep water temperatures cooler during warm weather. Rock salt is another additive that helps maintain the fish. And now there are commercially prepared elixirs manufactured by Jungle Laboratories, Box 630, Cibolo, Texas 78108, that will clean the livewell, remove ammonia buildup due to poor water quality or overcrowding, remove harmful chlorine, stop fungus, heal wounds and replace lost slime. They also produce a bait-saver treatment which keeps minnows alive and active on the hook up to ten times as long. These products were originally designed for the poor chaps who pursue bass and rockfish, but they're adaptable for our use.

Don't take the risk of spoiling a fine catch—layer the fish with layers of ice to insure proper cooling.

One word about coolers and ice......don't stack the fish in such a way that there's not some ice between top and bottom. A mass of fish in a cooler with ice on top of the heap may cause many to spoil before cleaning time. So keep them separated with layers of ice and drain the melted water off periodically. Otherwise, those that become submerged in water, even through cold, will lose some flavor.

I have left fish on ice overnight and cleaned them the next day but I think it's best to clean them as soon as possible—preferably before you leave the lake. Most marinas will have a fish-cleaning station that provides running water and the carcasses can be thrown into the water for turtles. Please don't clean fish on the launching ramps! It's unsightly, unhealthy, and creates a bad image for fishermen in the eyes of the boating public.

Now that the fish are caught, kept lively all day and photographed to show the boys at the office, it's time to clean them. And clean them all unless they're still alive and can be returned to the water. Don't catch more than you're going to clean even though they may never bite like this again. And don't catch a large number of fish with the justification that you'll give them to your neighbors. Number one, your neighbors will more than likely want them already cleaned and number two, unless they're elderly or bedridden, they don't deserve such largess. Tell them to catch their own!

There are two ways to clean a crappie—scaling or filleting. I grew up in the 40s, 50s, and even into the 60s and never once heard of filleting a fish. The only time you didn't eat the fish whole was when a big catfish was caught. He was skinned and cut into steaks for frying. Scaling was the only method for panfish in those days and I still prefer it on crappie if they're under a pound. The method is simple—take an old spoon or fish scaling tool, hold the fish by the head and work up the body from the tail. Be thorough and don't leave any scale that might appear later on someone's plate! That's known by the French as a *faux pas*!

After scaling, take a sharp knife and begin a cut behind the anal opening, between it and the fin, angle forward and downward through the body cavity toward the head. Keep the knife coming to the sharp edge of the gill plate, turn the fish on its side and sever around the gills to the backbone. Saw through the backbone and around the gills on the other side. Remove the viscera, clean the body cavity and the fish is ready for cooking. There's no need to cut off the fins or the tail. In fact there's real reason to leave them on! Both the dorsal and ventral fins are extremely handy when it comes time to eat the cooked, whole fish. By removing each fin prior to eating, the entire side of the fish can be laid off the spinal bones into one boneless piece with the exception of rib bones which can be easily removed. With this simple operation, people who are afraid of eating fish because of the bones, can now enjoy in calm assurance. Or, if they're still apprehensive, they can eat the tails which have no bones. When fried golden crispy, the tail is an outstanding "munchie." Besides, leaving the tail on makes the fish look bigger and discourages snide comments from the family about any resemblance to a minnow! Notice that I said discourage, not eliminate!

Fishermen in the 80s, however, want to fillet all of their catch—even the small crappie—and even bream! The method is quick and fairly efficient although some meat is lost. An excellent alternative is a combination of the two methods. Scale, then fillet one side and leave the other intact after removing the head.

Fillet knives come in all shapes and sizes and every cutlery company has one or more. Choose a well known brand and avoid the bargains. Berkley, Normark, Coleman, Gerber, Buck, and Case are just a few. A good fillet knife has to be maintained razor sharp for optimal results. Two knives are better than one, especially when there's more than 20 fish to be cleaned and the sharpening stone is somewhere else. Pictures in the text will demonstrate the mechanics of filleting. This is not the only way but it's as good as any. One ingredient to quality filleting is elevating the fish two or three inches off the table. Place a short 2 x 4 or 4 x 4 on the cleaning table to lay the fish on while filleting. The additional height allows you to perform the chore more efficiently and keeps the knife from digging into the table and dulling it prematurely. This is also true when using electric knives which are bigger and more awkward.

Electric fillet knives are the only way to go when cleaning large numbers of fish. And after reading this book, you'll be needing an electric! Don't make the mistake of using the family slicer. Buy your own. As in regular fillet knives, there are a lot of electric models but as of this writing, there are only three that are being marketed for filleting fish: the ELECTRIC FISHERMAN by MISTER TWISTER, INC. in Minden, Louisiana; RIVAL'S FILLETMASTER which has battery clips for running on 12 volt D.C. boat, car, or trolling motor batteries; and HAMILTON BEACH'S CORDLESS FILLET KNIFE which offers a rechargeable battery capable of filleting continuously for 30 minutes on full charge.

Most marinas, if they have a fish cleaning station, will have an electric outlet closeby to plug in an electric knife. During the spring crappie runs, the cleaning tables are a beehive of activity and places like Sportsman's Marina on Kentucky Lake will have a line of fishermen waiting their turn to get to the table. One guide service on this same lake (LAKELAND GUIDE SERVICE) insists on cleaning the catch at no extra charge to the customer. They also package the fillets in ziplock bags which are an essential item for the fisherman doing his own cleaning. The bags keep the fillets out of contact with water in the cooler. When you get home, add water to the bag and quick freeze. Another recommended medium for freezing crappie is milk cartons. They are readily available (all crappie fishermen drink sweet milk) and store easily in the freezer unit. Label with number of fish, date of catch, and the lake.

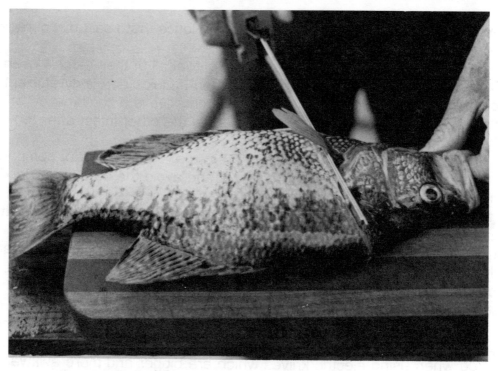

Angle the blade behind the gill down to the backbone.

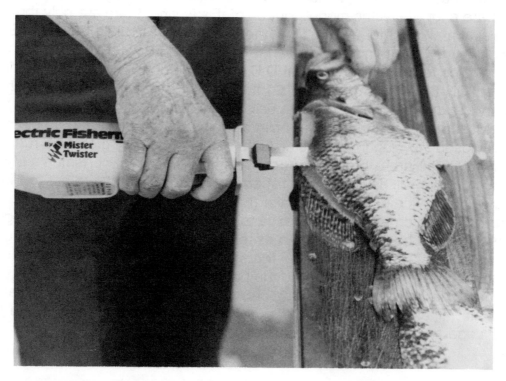

Turn the blade and cut toward the tail. Stay in contact with the backbone but be careful not to cut through it.

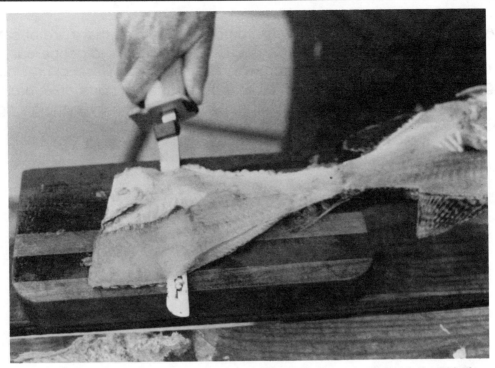

Flip the fillet before cutting through the tail and run the blade under the skin for the finished fillet.

Same procedure on the other side. The height of the cutting board makes it much easier to fillet.

Although there are as many ways to prepare them as there are of catching them, the Old South favorite is hard to beat: fillets salted and peppered, rolled in corn meal, and fried to a golden brown. The secret to this simple recipe is having the grease hot enough and knowing when they're done. Good old-fashioned cooks like my mother, well, they just know when everything's right. But what about us bachelors? We need guidelines. Recipes!

Recipes

FRIED CRAPPIE

2 cups yellow corn meal
1/2 cup flour
1 teaspoon black pepper
1 1/2 teaspoons paprika
1 tablespoon salt

Mix all ingredients together.
Dredge whole or filleted crappie in mixture.
Crappie should be moistened so mixture will adhere to fish.
Fry in deep hot oil until brown.

Gena Darnell, Kuttawa, Kentucky

MAYONNAISE CRAPPIE

Dry Fillets. Apply mayonnaise to both sides of fillet with a large pierced serving spoon. Sprinkle one side with coarsely ground black pepper, garlic powder (not salt) and paprika. Let stand one hour.

Cover grill (gas or charcoal) with HD aluminum foil—pierce foil. Place fillets on grill. Cook 10-15 minutes until fish appears firm and white. **Do not overcook!**

Serve with wild rice dressing and vinegar slaw.

Bob Holmes, Trenton, Tennessee

CRAPPIE a la WELBERN

Lay crappie fillets in pan lined with aluminum foil. Sprinkle on paprika and salt. Add lemon juice and a pat of butter on each piece. Save residue and place on table for dipping.

Cook in the oven at 350-375 degrees for about 20 minutes.

The only thing wrong with this recipe is that it takes about four more ounces of fish per person than when frying!

Serve with wild rice, baked potato and cole slaw.

John Welbern, Hendersonville, Tennessee

WICKER'S WALNUT CRAPPIE

Fillets (15-18) Soak overnight in salt water in refrigerator.
Make a mixture of 2/3 flour and 1/3 cracker crumbs.
Beat whites of 6 eggs until stiff.
6 to 8 ounces of black walnut pieces. Chop up fine.
Dip fillets in egg whites, then into flour and cracker crumb mixture and then into walnuts.
Melt 1/2 stick of butter in iron skillet. Add one tablespoon of oil to keep it from burning.
Put fillets in skillet and cook 3 or 4 minutes until brown.
Serve with hush puppies, vinegar slaw and your choice of potatoes.

Mrs. Scott Wicker, Kuttawa, Kentucky

HUSHPUPPIES

2 cups white corn meal
1 cup flour
2 tablespoons baking powder
1 1/2 teaspoon salt
1 teaspoon black pepper
1 cup diced onions (preferably green onions with tops)
1 cup beer

Mix all dry ingredients together, stir in onions. Add one cup of beer, mixing thoroughly.
Drop by heaping teaspoons into hot, deep, frying oil or shortening. Use the same oil that the fish were fried in.

Gena Darnell, Kuttawa, Kentucky

VINEGAR SLAW

Coarsely chop 1 small head of cabbage and 1 large onion into a bowl.
Add 1/4 cup vinegar, 1/8 cup salad oil, 1 teaspoon sugar, 1 tablespoon salad style mustard and 1/4 cup Wishbone Italian Dressing.
Season with coarsely ground black pepper, garlic powder or salt, paprika, celery seed and sweet pickle relish. Mix well.
Chill one hour in the refrigerator.

Bob Holmes, Trenton, Tennessee

WILD RICE DRESSING

2 boxes Uncle Ben's Original Long Grain & Wild Rice Mix.

Prepare per box instruction but substitute 1 can beef consomme' and 2 cans of chicken broth with equal volumes of water.

While rice cooks, coarsely chop 2 ribs of celery, 1/2 lb. fresh mushrooms and 1 medium Vidalia onion.

Fry 1/2 lb. smoked bacon until crisp. Remove bacon. Saute' chopped vegetables in bacon grease until onion is clear.

Combine rice, vegetables and crumbled bacon in large casserole dish.

Season with Louisiana Red Sauce (not Tabasco), black pepper, 1 teaspoon Worchestershire Sauce, light sprinkle of sage or poultry seasoning.

Bake 1 hours at 250 degrees covered. Bake uncovered if extra moisture is present.

Bob Holmes, Trenton, Tennessee

No fish dinner would be complete without dessert. Although most don't leave room for it, dinner guests never pass up an opportunity for a Lemon pie or Mrs. Robbins' Banana Pudding! If they do, it's usually gone when they go back to get it!

MRS. ROBBINS' BANANA PUDDING

2 eggs
1 cup sugar
2 tablespoons flour
2 cups sweet milk

Combine ingredients and heat in sauce pan on medium low heat.

When warm, dip out a small amount and add beaten egg yolks (two), stir and pour back into sauce pan (this keeps pudding smooth).

Stir constantly until desired thickness.

Layer vanilla wafers with alternate layer of sliced bananas to near the top of a large bowl. Add pudding and top with meringue!

Mrs. Sam Robbins, Memphis, Tennessee

LEMON SHAKER PIE

2 cups sugar
4 eggs, beaten
Pastry for two pie crusts

Slice 2 lemons paper thin, rind and all.
Mix in bowl with sugar.
Let stand two hours.

Line 9" pie plate with pastry. Add eggs to lemon mixture. Blend well and pour into pie crust. Cover with top crust and cut air vents. Crimp edges to prevent leaking and bake 15 minutes at 450 degrees. Reduce heat to 350 for 30 minutes or until a knife comes out clean.

Gena Darnell, Kuttawa, Kentucky